LONDON
A Visitors' Companion

LONDON
A Visitors' Companion

Charlotte & Denis Plimmer

W · W · NORTON & COMPANY · INC ·
NEW YORK

Published in the United States by
W. W. Norton & Company, Inc.

ISBN 0–393–04488–2
Printed in England

1   2   3   4   5   6   7   8   9   0

CONTENTS

LIST OF ILLUSTRATIONS

Maps and Plans

ACKNOWLEDGEMENTS

The authors and publishers would like to thank the following for permission to reproduce the photographs included in this book: the British Council, no. 31; the British Tourist Authority, nos. 10, 11, 15, 17, 37, 38, 40, 42, 57, 61, 65; J. Allan Cash Ltd, nos. 16, 35, 58; Claridge's, no. 48; the London Coliseum, no. 47; the Department of the Environment, no. 22; the Dorchester, no. 49; Eric de Maré, nos. 13, 32, 43; Fox Photos Ltd, no. 54; the Greater London Council, nos. 5, 36, 39, 41; A.F. Kersting, F.R.P.S., nos. 3, 6, 7, 9, 14, 19, 20, 21, 23, 25, 26, 27, 28, 30, 52, 59, 60, 62, 64; Bill Mackenzie, no. 51; National Monuments Record, nos. 12, 53, 56; National Theatre, no. 46; Publifotos, no. 55; Staniland Pugh, no. 4; the Savoy, no. 50; the late Alan Sorrell, no. 1; the late Edwin Smith, nos. 29, 34; John Stone, no. 24; Will Taylor, nos. 8, 33; Westminster Press Ltd, no. 2; Reg Wilson, no. 44.

For
Grace Garner
Who Chose London

I
FLOWER OF CITIES

SHORTLY before we began this book, we were asked to write a television play to be filmed in the streets of London. Our first task was to guide the camera towards all those small, insignificant and scarcely noticed trifles in the shifting scene of the capital which convey to the Londoner the feel, the smell, the ambience of his city – as it is now, in the last quarter of the twentieth century.

We started by listing a few visual snippets: a milkman bumping slowly along the street in his open-sided, battery-operated 'float'; a laundryman delivering the week's washing in a wicker basket to a housewife standing at the pink-painted door of her mews cottage; a 'crocodile' of small school-girls, four-in-hands neatly tied, straw boaters set square on their heads, crossing a road while a 'lollipop lady' holds the traffic back with her big round, long-handled STOP sign; the Blues glimpsed through the trees of Hyde Park, the plumes atop their helmets floating in the breeze as they ride towards the Horse Guards in Whitehall; a skyscraper hotel thrusting above the slated roofs of houses that were new when Queen Anne was on the throne; a leggy blonde entering Harrods; a King Charles spaniel managing to look dignified while cocking his leg against a red pillar box; a black cat in a greengrocer's window; the royal standard above Buckingham Palace.

London has always been considered a formal city, stately, its manners exquisite, even slightly frosty, its people aloof, taking their pleasures sadly. It has indeed its moments of splendid, unapproachable, almost glacial dignity, but these usually occur during those episodes of pageantry for which the English are justly world-famous. Yet, the greater the occasion, the warmer and more human the crowds become.

We recall standing in an endless queue on an icy day in the Victoria Gardens beside Parliament, waiting to enter Westminster Hall with thousands of others to pay our last respects to Sir Winston Churchill who lay in state there. The only sound in that lofty, echoing chamber when at last we passed inside was the susurrant shuffling of feet. But among the crowds there was quiet consideration towards each other. Youngsters gave their arms to old people, weary with waiting. Bowlered City men relieved exhausted mothers of their babies. The national family had lost a beloved member and, like all families, had drawn together, latent prejudices and selfishness forgotten in the presence of an overriding grief.

A few days later, during the funeral, we saw again this expression of the intuitive good taste of London. No one pushed, no one jostled as the gun-carriage and the troops slow-marched towards St Paul's. And afterwards, when the catafalque was borne from Tower Pier up the Thames to Waterloo, all the dozens of tall loading-cranes which line the river's banks gently lowered their tops, like sorrowing giants, towards the little vessel and its mighty cargo.

The muted pomp of that day became a dream of Empire passing, yet that silent, imaginative symbol of the mourning cranes remains as clear a picture in the mind as when they appeared that day against the grey and sombre sky.

In some cities – Paris and Washington, for instance – bricks and mortar, rather than people, set the mood. London's colour, like that of New York and Rome, owes more to its inhabitants than to its architects. Its millions surging through the big shopping streets and outdoor markets, climbing on and off the red double-decker buses, are swiftly responsive, quick to anger, equally quick to sympathize. Visitors are often surprised that Londoners, clichés and canards notwithstanding, are a talkative lot. Conversations bubble up with almost Latin volubility in bus queues, supermarkets, in the face of any sudden disaster. There are, of course, Englishmen who retire self-consciously behind their copies of *The Times* like shy rabbits nipping into their warrens at the approaching footsteps of a stranger. But even this increasingly rare species will emerge from hiding in time of trouble.

Not long ago our flat caught fire. We managed to escape inches ahead of the flames, carrying only our cat, Jocasta. Onlookers quickly gathered in the street, and, although there were the usual number of ghouls on hand to relish the smoke and the spread of the blaze, our neighbours, some of whom we knew but many of whom we did not, clustered about us like an impromptu Salvation Army as the fire engines roared up and the firemen rushed inside. One neighbour

brought whisky, another made tea, another, a doctor, produced tran-
quillizers. A lady whom we had always considered a bit stand-offish
took Jocasta into her care. When it became clear that our flat would be
uninhabitable for months, two more neighbours offered us theirs,
rent-free.

The incident – so nearly a tragedy – reflected faithfully the compas-
sion of this people whom London and its history have made, shaped
and tempered over the centuries since Rome's legionaries, on leave
from their frontier posts, swaggered in to the Thames-side fortress
settlement to drink the wine and see the bright lights.

Little of Roman London is visible today outside museums, save for
brief stretches of the old wall which girdled the City, and the reconstructed remains of a second-century temple to the sun god, Mithras,
favourite of the legions, a few yards from the lord mayor's Mansion
House. But the blood of ancient Rome still courses through the veins
of the modern Londoner. It has always been our own personal theory
that the Roman heritage is far more genetic than archaeological. Most
people think of the Englishman as tall, slim and blond. This type
exists in great numbers, of course, and derives chiefly from the later
Scandinavian invasions. Many Londoners, however, are short, stocky
and dark, like modern Romans. Their personalities, as we have said,
are similar too, as is their love of music, colour, flowers, display. To us
the reason is clear: they are descendants of all those Flaviuses and
Marcuses who came to *Londinium* to build and to breed and to create
what Tacitus, in the first century AD, described as 'a town of the
highest repute and a busy emporium of trade and traders'.

Listen to Alfred Noyes on the subject:

. . . Verdi, Verdi, when you wrote *Il Trovatore*, did you dream
    Of the City when the sun sinks low,
Of the organ and the monkey and the many-coloured stream
On the Piccadilly pavement, of the myriad eyes that seem
To be litten for a moment with a wild Italian gleam
As *A che la morte* parodies the world's eternal theme
    And pulses with the sunset-glow?

London, like most old European cities, is a palimpsest of many ages,
but not a great deal is left that pre-dates the end of the seventeenth
century. Much of the London we know was formed by Christopher
Wren after the Great Fire of 1666, which destroyed four-fifths of the
City – more than 13,000 houses, 44 livery companies, 86 parish churches
and old St Paul's Cathedral. A large section further to the west was
firmly stamped by John Nash, under the Prince Regent. The London

of the earlier Georges and little patches of Queen Anne's, as well, persist in handsome squares and crescents. But just as the Stuart Age swept away the London of the Plantagenets, and the Hanovers super-imposed upon the Stuarts, so the Victorians eradicated miles of the London of 'Farmer George'. And the twentieth-century's money-conscious speculators have done far more damage to the older and more comely quarters of the capital than Goering's *Luftwaffe* did.

Although more of old London has been deliberately destroyed since World War I than in any previous century, Londoners today talk far more of architectural conservation than ever in their history. There are groups to preserve Georgian London, Victorian London, even Edwardian London. The result is sometimes stalemate. Plans to re-habilitate Piccadilly Circus have proliferated so richly over the past 30 years and cancelled each other out so regularly that the Circus remains substantially as it was in the 1930s, if more rundown, more raffish and perhaps less endearing. Yet, while the Circus's attackers and defenders continue to hold each other at bay, developers have cut vast and cruel swathes through the gentle green squares of Bloomsbury; skyscrapers have fringed Hyde Park, and the cherished vista down St James's Street to the Tudor palace at its foot has been violated by a monolithic office building rising against the sky beyond.

Despite the English reverence for antiquity, it is obvious that since the capital's real estate is worth a great deal of money, those who own it are bound to maximize the profits they can wring from it. *The Sunday Times* recently observed that London is 'an unmanageable honeycomb of communities, a jumble of conflicting needs, of historical accidents and of economic necessities, whose perspective shifts every time you blink'.

Yet out of this discordant, tumbling twentieth-century sea of urbanism, roiled and roughened by planners, politicians, property developers and architects, a series of immutable islets survive against whose craggy walls the hopes of the demolition men dash in vain. These are the serene fortresses of the spirit of this ancient stronghold – the Abbey, St Paul's, St James's, Kensington and Buckingham Palaces, the Tower, the Nash terraces adjoining Regent's Park, Lincoln's Inn and the Temple, Lambeth Palace, Trafalgar Square. The visitor heads for these supreme examples of what the Germans call *Sehenswert*; the Londoner himself tends not so much to ignore them as to take them for granted. They lurk, however, in the innermost recesses of his mind and generate his own personal city climate. It is enough that he knows they are there, fixed moons in his particular cosmos.

London, Churchill once said, could absorb and nullify an entire

1 *above* Roman London in the third century A.D.

2 *right* Excavation of the Roman wall discovered near Blackfriars Bridge

1   Kensington Palace
2   Albert Memorial
3   Albert Hall
4   Science Museum
5   Geological Museum
6   Natural History Museum
7   West London Air Terminal
8   Victoria and Albert Museum
9   Brompton Oratory
10 Crosby Hall
11 Carlyle's House
12 Chelsea Hospital
13 Festival Gardens
14 Lord's Cricket Ground
15 Zoological Gardens
16 Planetarium and Tussaud's Waxworks
17 Wallace Collection
18 Roosevelt Statue, Grosvenor Square
19 Buckingham Palace
20 St James's Palace
21 Westminster Cathedral
22 Tate Gallery

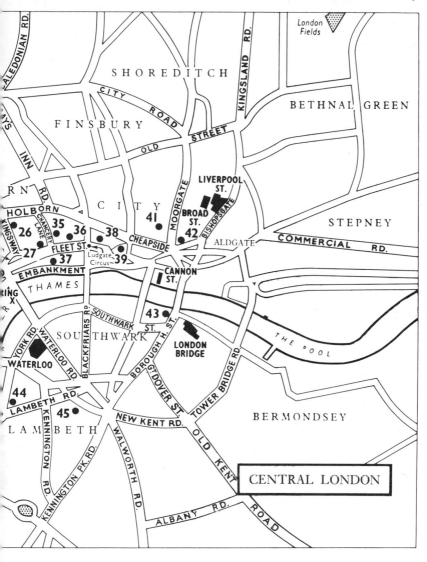

CENTRAL LONDON

23 Courtauld Institute Gallery
24 London University
25 British Museum
26 Sir John Soane Museum
27 Law Courts
28 National Gallery
29 National Portrait Gallery
30 Horse Guards
31 No. 10 Downing Street
32 Banqueting House
33 Westminster Abbey
34 Houses of Parliament
35 Public Record Office
36 Dr Johnson's House
37 The Temple
38 Old Bailey
39 St Paul's
40 Wellington Museum (Apsley House)
41 Guildhall
42 Bank, Mansion House, Royal Exchange
43 Southwark Cathedral
44 Lambeth Palace
45 Imperial War Museum

German army by itself, its people fighting street by street. It is true that, unlike much of Paris and virtually all of New York, London is a bad city for set-piece battles. It is, instead, perfect guerilla terrain. Its very enormousness and its acres of convoluted planlessness would drive a conventionally-minded general to madness. Streets unexpectedly become cul-de-sacs; lanes and alleys dart off avenues; crescents spawn baby crescents. There are 6,000 miles of public way, but few thoroughfares are in any normal sense throughways.

To make matters even more complex, the same street, as one geographical region yields to the next, may change its name half a dozen times. The main east–west artery, beginning from the Mansion House, where it is called Poultry, becomes successively Cheapside, Newgate Street, Holborn Viaduct, Holborn, New Oxford Street, Oxford Street, the Bayswater Road, Notting Hill Gate, Holland Park Avenue, the Uxbridge Road and on with more name-changes through a string of suburbs into rural Buckinghamshire.

The confusion is worse confounded by the fact that the same name – often that of one of the great landowning families, past or present – may appear in a multiplicity of guises. The Cadogan family are commemorated not only in Chelsea, a large chunk of which they have owned (or still own) and which is referred to as the Cadogan Estate, but elsewhere in London. There are, besides four different Cadogan Gardens, Cadogan Lane, Cadogan Gate, Cadogan Pier, Cadogan Place, Cadogan Road, Cadogan Square and Cadogan Terrace. Portland appears 32 times, Bedford, 49 and Grosvenor, 77. When George Villiers, the second Duke of Buckingham sold off a parcel of land between the Strand and the river, he stipulated that streets there perpetuate both his full name and his title. So, there were George Court, Villiers Street, Duke Street, Of Alley and Buckingham Street.

How evocative London names can be: Old Jewry, Shepherd's Bush, Bleeding Heart Yard, Half Moon Street, Strutton Ground, the Elephant and Castle, Whitechapel, Hanging Sword Alley, Seacoal Lane, Adam and Eve Mews, Threadneedle Street, Crutched Friars, Well Walk, Apothecary Street, Frying Pan Alley, Knightsbridge.

What is it like to live in modern London, in an average residential neighbourhood? Take our own, a small enclave on the eastern edge of Paddington known informally as Little Venice. One of many London 'villages' with strongly individual personalities, it is made up of a dozen or so streets which border or run into the Regent's Canal. The area is not historically noteworthy, although John Nash built a stretch of the canal, Robert Browning lived on its south bank (and wrote *The*

Ring and the Book there) and Sir John Tenniel, who illustrated *Alice in Wonderland*, lived near the north bank. Architecturally it is a hodge-podge, everything from drab contemporary council houses to glistening white canal-side mansions in the Regency manner, many of which are inhabited by the titled, the distinguished and/or the wealthy. The tributary streets, broad and tree-lined, consist largely of cream-coloured, classically-designed four- and five-storey houses. Built during Victoria's reign for well-to-do merchants, they have a certain modest nobility.

In the 1930s Little Venice went downhill socially, and many of its streets, especially what was then called Portsdown Road, became the haunts of prostitutes who lived in furnished bed-sitters. After a couple of decades, the Commissioners of the Church of England, which owns the property, decided to rehabilitate the region. Out went the prostitutes and out even the old name. Portsdown Road was changed to Randolph Avenue (after a forgotten bishop) in an attempt to exorcise the demons of commercial vice. The prostitutes were succeeded by a conglomeration of immigrants of varied colours and nationalities.

But the wind of change was still gusting. By the 1960s, with an ever-increasing demand for housing in central London, the commissioners began one by one to convert the Victorian residences, their paintwork scrofulous with age, weather and neglect, to middle-class apartments. As the builders and decorators moved in, the immigrants sadly drifted away.

The present incumbents are, for the most part, professional people – doctors, solicitors, barristers, TV and stage actors, journalists, authors, architects – the sort who a few years back would have lived in Chelsea or Kensington, before high rents drove them forth into what the dwellers of Knightsbridge, Belgravia *et al* consider the wilderness north of Hyde Park. Perhaps because all of us who live here are refugees of a sort (the most contemporary sort – in flight from economic pressures), we have in the brief years since our coming formed a remarkably close-knit community. We exchange dinner parties, baby-sit for each other, commiserate over the stresses of urban married life, serve together on garden committees, have mild flirtations with each other, do each other's shopping, and borrow each other's cooking utensils, to say nothing of the odd fiver. The neighbourhood is predominately British, but, as in most London middle-class areas, well-salted with other nationalities – American, Dutch, Indian, Swiss, Argentine, New Zealand, Australian, Danish.

For 'serious' shopping, the wives turn to the big department stores and supermarkets in or near Oxford Street and the rest of the West

3 Cumberland Terrace, Regent's Park

End. For recherché foods, they go to the Continental and Oriental shops in Soho, and for culinary bargains, to the nearby open-air market in Church Street. But 90 per cent of what they need from day to day is supplied by a small string of merchants in the Clifton Road, which parallels the Canal and comes to its end in Maida Vale, the northward extension of the Edgware Road.

None of these local establishments (except for several that belong to national chains) is in a large way of business. There are four grocers, one with a 'gourmet' section, a delicatessen; a newsagent-cum-bookseller; a florist; a confectioner; a bakery; two each of butchers, dress boutiques, pubs, greengrocers, estate agents, wine merchants and chemists; a tobacconist; a post office; a fishmonger; an ironmonger, and a small and friendly Italian restaurant. Most of the shopkeepers know most of the customers by name, keep track of their babies and their various ailments and conduct client relations on a basis of easy chatty domesticity.

Many ground-floor flats in Little Venice have private gardens of their own. Dwellers higher up more often than not look out on large communal gardens, completely hidden from the street, to which their tenancy entitles them to keys. London probably has more green space than any other major city in the world. Ten per cent of the entire metropolitan spread – some 30,000 acres in all – is given over to gigantic public parks. There are 1,200 acres more of tree-shaded squares. But in many ways, the 'secret' interior gardens, often overgrown and unmanicured, which are peculiar to the areas north of Hyde Park, are the most welcoming of all.

A country child, brought to central London for the first time, stared in wonder at the crowds, the traffic, the big stores and the electric signs. Finally she asked a devastating question: 'Daddy, what is London for?'

He was completely stumped, as most people would be, for London, though the least purpose-built town we know, has a bewildering multiplicity of purposes. Getting and spending are almost certainly the chief ones, but this bitter tandem of human motivations is incarnated in many forms and expresses many strange and unlikely ambitions, not only on the part of Londoners, but among those who for one reason or another seek the city out.

We once knew a Scot who came to apprentice himself to a Camden Town bagpipe-maker. We have known girls who came to find husbands, and at least one husband who came to divorce his wife – not that this is particularly easy, but at least the lawyers know their business. We have met dozens of Africans, Asians and Continentals who have come to study in its universities.

Americans seem to have the weirdest reasons of all for visiting London. A Californian travelled some 6,000 miles just to buy a violin bow in Bond Street. A Chicago sewage engineer arrived to study the 'lost' underground rivers. A lady lawyer from Kansas City wanted an English barrister's wig, to wear at home for a giggle. A Texas golfer came to find a pukka Raj-type solar topee to keep the sun off as he sweated around his home course. A private eye from Seattle yearned only to investigate the East End haunts of Jack the Ripper.

That so many disparate desires can be satisfied is merely a minor measure of London's capabilities. London is today the acknowledged international centre of musical performance, of the theatre and of the art market. The Great Ormond Street Hospital for Sick Children is one of the two or three leading hospitals of its kind anywhere. The capital is also a major force in other branches of medicine, especially in transplant surgery and in the treatment of mental, cardiac and tropical diseases.

4 Lincoln's Inn

The British Museum Library is rivalled only by the Library of Congress in Washington and the Bibliothèque Nationale in Paris; and the borough public-library system is entirely without equal. The Stock Exchange is runner-up to New York's. London is supreme in innumerable branches of commerce and trade: insurance, furs, tea, spices, international freight, gold, diamonds. It shares with New York top position in the ready-to-wear rag trade and in pop music. Lord's is the mecca of world cricket, and Wimbledon of tennis. And where else but in London can the connoisseur find precisely the kind of pub he likes best?

The poets, also, have been generous in their praise. Wordsworth, of course, thought nothing on earth more fair than the view from Westminster Bridge. Masefield liked the sights, the ale and the 'brisk' air. Sir John Betjeman has praised London's Victoriana. And William Dunbar, 500 years ago, came down from Scotland to find, as so many Scots have done, a vision of perfection:

London, thou art the flower of cities all,
Gem of all joy, jasper of jocundity.

5 Little Venice

Another Scot, Ian Mackay, the late revered columnist of the late revered *News Chronicle*, also had London pride. When he learned on 15 July 1950, that London had become the biggest city in the world (Tokyo has outstripped it since), he went in and out of Fleet Street pubs, buttonholing Americans, fixing them with his glittering Caledonian eye and growling fiercely, 'Whaur's your Manhattan noo?'

Dickens understood London better than most writers, but his love affair with the city, though long lasting, rarely ran smooth. Most of the time he was in a fearful temper with it. But the British have always deprecated what was their own.

Only when a Londoner is abroad does he suddenly discover civic pride. A Cockney who found himself in Canada during World War II was asked by an official where he was born.

'London.'

'London?' demanded the man dim-wittedly, 'London where? London, Ontario? New London, Connecticut?'

The Cockney replied with withering dignity, 'London, the whole bloody world!'

II
THE TOWER
OF LONDON

ONE CALM summer's evening we drove eastward from the pleasure-seeking, self-indulgent West End to Tower Hill. As we moved from the Strand along Fleet Street to St Paul's, the streets, so crammed by by day with City office workers, grew quieter, almost deserted. We parked at the brow of Tower Hill beneath an apple-green sky. The windows were dark in the new business blocks that now rise anachronistically in this ancient setting. The time-worn silhouette of the Tower of London glimmered whitely in the dying twilight, battlements and turrets juxtaposed as in a child's dream castle. Here and there lights flickered behind narrow arrow-slits, beckoning and oddly mysterious. It was a quarter to ten.

At the gate a yeoman warder in blue undress uniform challenged us. We produced a slip of paper that had come in the post that morning. 'We have the governor's permission to see "the Keys".' He glanced at the chit and waved us on. 'You'll be met at the Byward Tower.'

We passed under the arch of the Middle Tower which guards the causeway over the moat and walked beneath the portcullis of the thirteenth-century Byward Tower. A second yeoman warder motioned us to stand to one side. A door in the tower opened. It was precisely seven minutes to ten.

The chief warder, a tall figure in long scarlet coat and Tudor bonnet, stepped out. In one hand he carried a lantern, lit by a stumpy tallow candle. In the other he held a ring of heavy iron keys. The ceremonial locking of the Tower of London against all intruders was about to begin, a nightly ritual that has persisted almost unbroken for seven centuries.

The Tower of London is the largest and oldest continuously-

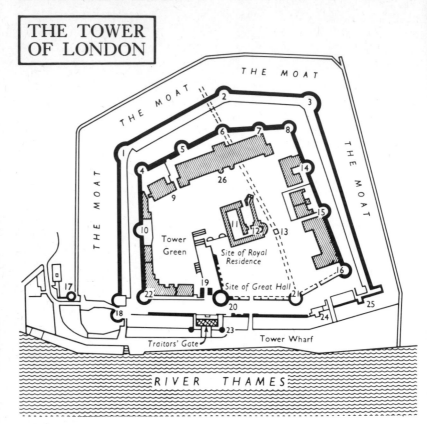

THE TOWER
OF LONDON

1 Legge's Mount	14 Constable Tower
2 North Bastion	15 Broad Arrow Tower
3 Brass Mount	16 Salt Tower
4 Devereux Tower	17 Middle Tower
5 Flint Tower	18 Byward Tower
6 Bowyer Tower	19 Bloody Tower
7 Brick Tower	20 Wakefield Tower
8 Martin Tower	21 Lanthorn Tower
9 St Peter ad Vincula	22 Bell Tower
10 Beauchamp Tower	23 St Thomas's Tower
11 White Tower and Armoury	24 Cradle Tower
12 St John's Chapel	25 Well Tower
13 Wardrobe Tower and Roman Wall	26 Waterloo Barracks (Crown Jewels)

occupied military fortress in the western world. William the Conqueror's Norman builder, Gundulf, Bishop of Rochester, began in 1078 to construct its keep, the massive White Tower with its four jaunty little pinnacles, which is the pivot of the entire complex. In succeeding reigns over the next 400 years the inner and outer walls were created, with 13 towers emplaced at strategic points in the former, and six more in the latter to stand sentinel by the moat. Two last bastions, at the north-west and north-east corners, were added by Henry VIII.

William created the Tower chiefly to protect London from foreign attack by way of the River Thames: in Saxon days Vikings and Norsemen had several times sent waterborne forces, and the Conqueror was determined that no one should wrest from him what he himself had taken. He also needed protection against Londoners who did not take kindly to his conquest. The Tower became a royal palace, the seat of government, a prison, the vast protective strongbox which contains the Crown Jewels.

The chief warder now about-faced and marched along Water Lane, a passage between the inner and the outer walls. As the light of his lantern flickered into the distance, we were signed to follow him. He halted at the Bloody Tower and called, 'Escort for the Keys!'

Four guardsmen turned out, smart in their busbies and scarlet tunics. Three held rifles at the slope. The warder handed his lantern to the fourth and marched back towards the outside gate through which he had just entered. Sentries presented arms as the Keys were carried under the shadowy arches. Martial footsteps echoed hollowly. At the main gate the escort stood to attention as the chief warder turned the key that closed the Tower off from the outside world. They swung back again to lock first the heavy oaken doors of the Middle Tower and then those of the Byward Tower. The little procession, the lantern bobbing ahead, now returned to the Bloody Tower and stopped at its entry, challenged by a sentry.

'Halt. Who comes there?'

'The Keys.'

'Whose Keys?'

'Queen Elizabeth's Keys.'

'Advance, Queen Elizabeth's Keys. All's well.'

We were now enclosed within the innermost of the Tower's defences. A ramp led upwards towards a brief flight of stone steps. To our right Gundulf's keep glimmered whitely. At the top of the ramp stood the main guard in dress scarlet, an officer before them, his sword bared.

'Guard and escort, present arms!'

7 St John's Chapel, White Tower

The escort snapped their rifles to the 'present' position. Steel flickered as the officer lifted his sword. It was now a few seconds before ten o'clock. The chief warder stepped forward and raised his Tudor bonnet.

'God preserve Queen Elizabeth.'

There was a rumble of voices from the guard. 'Amen.'

As the chimes of ten began, the bugler raised his instrument and the slow sweet notes of 'The Last Post' stole across the open space and rang back from the heavy walls that overhung us. The music and the chimes ceased simultaneously. It was a moment of singular beauty.

The Tower of London stands on rising ground between Tower Hill and the river. There was once a belief, fostered among others by Shakespeare whose scholarship fell far short of his poetry, that it was built by Julius Caesar. Caesar never even came to Londinium. However the Romans, like the Conqueror a thousand years later, had recognized that the site was defensively important. Scraps of Roman masonry have been found to the east of the White Tower, suggesting that early fortifications overlooked the river; near where they were unearthed, a corner of the wall with which the Romans surrounded their square-mile city still survives.

To consolidate his kingdom, William threw up a circle of fortresses around the capital, some of which, at Rochester and Guildford, for instance, remain. The most important then as now were Windsor Castle and the Tower. By the time Columbus set sail for the New World, these two had housed 19 English kings. The Tower was the chief London residence for most of them until the Tudors. Sovereigns, their families and their noble courtiers lived on the top two floors of the White Tower; their personal servants and household troops occupied the floors below, and beneath them were the dungeons. By the thirteenth century, the royal living space had spread over a cluster of buildings that connected the central keep with the Lanthorn Tower on the inner wall. Here the king had his bedchamber and closet, overlooking private gardens.

Oliver Cromwell, in a burst of egalitarian zeal, destroyed this regal housing development, but he kept his hands off the towers. It was Charles II who had the Lanthorn Tower torn down, and substituted for it a clumsy ordnance-storage shed. The present tower is a nineteenth-century reproduction of the original, build by command of Queen Victoria.

Cromwell need not have been quite so zealous, for by his time the royal association with the riverside fortress was already wearing thin.

In the 1530s, Henry VIII, finding his existing quarters in the Tower too cramped, had started work on a new mini-palace tucked into the south-west corner of the inner wall. But before it was completed, he formed a passion for two other dwellings, Cardinal Wolsey's Hampton Court, and the cardinal's Westminster seat, Whitehall. Bluff King Hal elbowed the cardinal aside and took them both over. At about the same time, he began to build still another residence, St James's Palace.

He never lived in his new Tower home, a comfortable half-timbered three-storey building, now called Queen's House, from whose front door Tower Green stretches northwards to the little chapel of St Peter ad Vincula. Henry's house became first the 'Lieutenant's Lodgings', assigned to the officer in charge of prisoners, and later, the home of the resident governor.

It was in Queen's House, where the Keys are safely secreted nightly, that we recently met the present governor, Major-General W.D.M. Raeburn of the Scots Guards. Because it is his private residence, this, the most homelike building in the fortress, is not open to visitors. This is a pity, for Queen's House is resonant with overtones.

General Raeburn directs the Tower's manifold affairs from a roomy but unpretentious office on the ground floor. On one wall hangs the handsome, brass-studded Tudor axe which was always borne ceremonially before a condemned prisoner when he was brought back by barge after his trial at Westminster. If the sentence was death, the sharp edge was carried facing towards him. The return was usually through the Traitor's Gate, the only direct entrance from the river. The portcullis was raised – it is still in working order – and the condemned man or woman landed within the walls to await the scaffold.

Until the 1960s, the Tower was a fully garrisoned fortress. Though the troops have moved elsewhere, the military flavour persists, and the governor is always a senior officer with an impressive record. General Raeburn was formerly C-in-C, Allied Forces, Northern Europe. Under his control are 37 yeomen warders, all beribboned campaign veterans; a number of guardsmen seconded from the five regiments who make up the brigade of guards; a mixed bag of maintenance experts, archaeologists, antiquarians, armourers, security men, museum attendants and the famous ravens that stalk Tower Green.

The present feathered complement is eight. These black predatory birds have been 'on the establishment' since Charles II's reign, when a legend began that if the ravens were ever to desert the Tower, the Empire would collapse. Well, the Empire has disintegrated, but the cruel-beaked birds are still there, wings clipped so they can't fly away, fed and pampered by a yeoman warder.

The general led us to an oblong chamber on the top floor of Queen's House, where King James I's privy councillors interrogated Guy Fawkes. Sunshine poured through the windows and across the long polished oak table. He then showed us a small, comfortable bedroom down one flight, overlooking the green. 'They kept Anne Boleyn here', he said. 'There are some scratches in the stone mantel that she made – or was said to have made.' Her jailer was the then constable of the Tower, Sir William Kingston, who, with his wife beside him, slept outside her door throughout the 18 nights she was imprisoned, so that they could hear everything she said to the women who attended her.

From this room Anne wrote to Henry VIII beseeching him to spare the four men he had clapped into the Tower on the charge that they had been her lovers, and asking that she alone 'bear the burden of your Grace's displeasure'. She concluded touchingly, 'If ever I have found favour in your sight, if ever the name of Anne Boleyn hath been pleasing in your ears, then let me obtain this request; and I will so leave off troubling your Grace any further, with mine earnest prayers to the Trinity to have your Grace in his good keeping, and to direct you in all your actions. From my doleful prison in the Tower, this 6th of May. Your most loyal and ever faithful wife, Anne Boleyn.'

She could achieve no more for her putative lovers than for herself or for her brother, with whom she was accused of having committed incest. All were condemned to die. On the eve of her execution she sent a last message to Henry, again protesting her innocence and thanking him for his favours. He had, she wrote, first raised her to a marchioness, then to a queen, and now he was sending her to be a saint. She also asked him to care for their infant daughter, Elizabeth. Shortly before she was led to the headsman's block, Kingston assured her that she would feel no pain. She placed her fingers around her throat and laughed. 'I have heard say the executioner is very good, and I have a little neck.' The next day, her widower married Jane Seymour.

As for the infant Elizabeth, she too was eventually to be committed to the Tower. Four years before she reached the throne, her half-sister, Mary, imprisoned her on the suspicion of treason. Mary had succeeded following the death, at 16, of their brother, Edward VI, and the abortive tenure of Lady Jane Grey. Mary feared her formidable sister far more than she had her gentle cousin.

General Raeburn opened a small door at the end of a corridor and showed us the room in which Elizabeth was held. It is in the upper storey of one of the oldest bastions, the Bell Tower, and is accessible only through Queen's House. Roughly circular and lighted by arrow-slits cut into walls some eight feet thick, it is a grim uncompromising cell. So confining did the princess find it that after a few weeks her health began to fail, and she was permitted to walk along the ramparts as far as Beauchamp Tower, a bleak parade still known as 'Elizabeth's Walk'. She came to detest the Tower, and, as queen, never lived in it.

In the chamber below Elizabeth's, Sir (now Saint) Thomas More, Henry VIII's lord chancellor, had languished 20 years earlier. Imprisoned for refusing to condone Henry's revolt against the Roman Catholic religion and his divorce of his first queen, Katharine of Aragon, he was held for 15 months during which he remained adamant in his faith. Finally he was executed. As he mounted the scaffold, he said to an onlooker, 'Friend, help me up, and when I come down again, let me shift for myself.' Before he laid his head on the block, he forgave his executioner, and then he thrust his beard to one side so that the axe should not touch it. It deserved no punishment, he said, for it had 'never committed treason'.

The block was always placed (the spot is now marked) towards the northern end of Tower Green, near the chapel of St Peter ad Vincula. To the left, between the Beauchamp Tower and Queen's House, is a row of simple houses in one of which the gentleman jailer used to live. From this little dwelling – or rather from a Tudor predecessor on the same site – Lady Jane Grey, the queen-for-nine-days, was led across the few yards of greensward to the scaffold.

Lady Jane, a modest, retiring, scholarly girl, came to the throne reluctantly. As the cousin of young Edward VI, she stood in the succession behind both his half-sisters, Mary and Elizabeth. But Jane was married to Lord Guildford Dudley, whose power-hungry father, the Duke of Northumberland, convinced the boy-king as he lay dying to bypass his sisters and bequeath the crown to Jane. Mary moved quickly to arrest Northumberland, Dudley, Jane and Jane's father, the Duke of Suffolk. All were tried and sentenced to be executed for high treason. Jane was 17, her husband 18.

Not long before her beheading, the doomed girl wrote an inscription for the lieutenant of the Tower in his book of devotions. It closed with these words: 'As the preacher sayeth, there is a time to be born and a time to die; and the day of death is better than the day of our birth'. The young couple's ending was made even more poignant by the fact that they were to die separately, he outside the walls on Tower Hill, she shortly afterwards on the Green.

Dudley begged for a last meeting, but Jane, fearing that they might both break down, refused him. 'Tell him', she said, 'that our separation is but momentary, and that we shall soon meet in Heaven, where our love will know no interruption, and where our joys and felicities will be for ever and ever.' She stood at a window and waved as he was escorted away. She was still at the window when his headless body was borne back in a cart. And then it was her turn.

At the scaffold her lady attendants removed her outer robes and handed her 'a fair handkerchief to bind about her eyes'. She knelt before the block and calmly blindfolded herself, then reached forward groping, 'What shall I do? Where is it? Where is it?' Someone guided her hands and she lay her neck on the wood. As she prayed, 'Into Thy hands, Lord, I commend my spirit', the axe came down. She was buried in St Peter ad Vincula beside her husband, and a few feet to the west of Anne Boleyn.

Dudley had been held in the Beauchamp Tower, one of the most powerful bastions of all. Flat on the side that faces the green, it bulges powerfully on the opposite side out towards the moat. Its walls crawl with signatures and observations cut into the stone by noble prisoners. Among these the name 'Jane' appears, quite possibly incised by the heartbroken Dudley. Was it when he received her message as the morning light entered his cell – the light of his last morning on earth – that he carved that touching and pathetic 'Jane'?

The Devereux Tower, at the north-western corner of the inner wall, was named after the reckless fiery Robert Devereux, second Earl of Essex, the man whom Queen Elizabeth once loved – and perhaps still loved when she imprisoned him there. One of those brilliant human comets who light up the sky of a nation's political and military life, Essex's descent was as dazzlingly quick as his rise, and ended on the block when he was only 34. He had been a general, a privy councillor, the earl marshal, chancellor of Cambridge University and so much the queen's favourite that it was he who walked by her side, holding the rein, whenever she rode in stately procession.

But bit by bit he managed to annoy her. Against her will he sailed with Drake to attack Portugal. Against her will he married Sir Philip Sydney's widow. When Elizabeth commanded him to quell the rebellion in Ireland, he failed, and returned to London against orders. All this, together with reliable reports that he had had illicit relations with various court ladies, disenchanted the queen. Yet Essex still carried a ring she had given him during the days when in her eyes he could do no wrong. If ever, she had told him, he were in danger, he was to send the ring and she would come to his aid.

After the Irish fiasco, Essex was stripped of his honours. Fuming in retirement outside London, he concocted a rebellious coup that involved kidnapping the queen. But the plot was discovered, he was confined in the Tower and sentenced to be hanged, drawn and quartered.

For days, Elizabeth agonized over whether or not to sign the execution warrant, hoping against hope that Essex would send the ring. It is believed that he finally did – by way of the influential Countess of Nottingham whose husband, as lord high admiral, had commanded the triumphant forces against the Spanish Armada. Nottingham, so the story goes, advised his wife not to pass the ring on. After Essex was dead, the countess confessed to the queen that they had withheld it. Elizabeth replied furiously, 'God may forgive you, but I never can.' She had not long to bear her grudge; she was then 68 and only two years from her own death.

The Martin Tower, at the north-eastern corner of the inner wall, also held its share of distinguished inmates. But it is best remembered as the scene of Colonel Blood's bizarre attempt in 1671 to steal the crown jewels, which in those days were kept in a vaulted chamber on the tower's ground floor. Blood was a mystery man, but he had proved earlier that he was a rogue. He had long held a grievance against the Marquess of Ormonde, who, when he had been Charles II's lord lieutenant in Ireland, had executed some of Blood's cohorts after they had conspired to seize Dublin Castle.

Blood himself managed to get to London, but his family's Irish estates were confiscated in reprisal for his part in the castle imbroglio. He became a well-known figure among the fashionable roisterers of St James's, and worked out a plan for revenge: to kidnap Ormonde, drag him to Tyburn and hang him. One December night in 1670 Blood and five accomplices attacked him as he rode home in his carriage. Ormonde, though he was by then 60, managed to fight them off, and they fled into the darkness. A reward of £1,000 was offered for their capture, and although it was suspected that Blood was involved, he was not arrested. The fact that it was he who had instigated the crime did not emerge until after his exploit at the Martin Tower.

He had laid the groundwork carefully. The jewels were in the care of a 77-year old deputy keeper, Talbot Edwards, who lived above the shop, so to speak. He was permitted to unlock the great chamber below when visitors wanted to see the treasure, and to keep for himself whatever tips he could cadge. Blood disguised himself as a parson, and took to dropping in from time to time to have a look at the jewels. He won Edwards's confidence completely, and was soon suggesting a marriage between the old man's daughter and an invented nephew of his own. The 'parson' promised to bring the 'nephew' at seven a.m.

a few days later so that the couple could meet.

The men arrived on time with two friends. The daughter, however, was still upstairs primping, and Blood suggested that they see the regalia while they waited. As soon as the old man unlocked the door, the foursome struck him on the head and gagged him. Blood snatched the State Crown and hammered it flat with a mallet to make it easier to carry. Two of his accomplices snatched the Orb and the Sceptre, and they all ran hell for leather.

But while they were still in the Tower precincts, Edwards's son, a soldier home from the war in Flanders, arrived unexpectedly, found his father unconscious and saw that the treasury was rifled. He began to shout, the garrison turned out and there was a chase towards the south-east exit. Leading the pursuers was the 'parson', shouting 'Stop thief!' at the top of his voice. But he was arrested with the others, just as they were about to leap into their saddles.

What followed has never been explained. Charles II decided to question Blood personally, and the culprit confessed everything – not only the theft and the attack on Ormonde, but even the fact that he had conspired to shoot the king one day when he was swimming in the Thames near Battersea. Blood had withheld his fire, he said, 'because he was struck with so great an awe' when he beheld his majesty in his gun-sight.

When Charles asked him how he could have dared to steal the jewels, he replied, 'My father lost a good estate for the crown, and I considered it no crime to recover it from the crown.' The king then asked, 'What if I should give you your life?' Blood said calmly, 'I should try to deserve it.' Not only was he forgiven, both by Charles and by Ormonde, but he was appointed to the king's bodyguard and given a pension of £500 a year.

Why should Charles have been so preposterously indulgent? Was he, as many believe, enchanted by the sheer swaggering impudence of the man? Or was it that, perennially hard up for cash, he himself had actually commissioned Blood to steal the jewels and sell them on his behalf? Romantics prefer the former interpretation, cynics (and Cromwellians) the latter.

The casual attitude towards the crown jewels that the Blood story reveals was nothing new. One early monarch kept them in a box under his bed. At various other times they were held in palaces outside London, or put in the charge of the king's treasurer or of the abbot of Westminster Abbey. On several occasions they were pledged in exchange for loans. When Cromwell came along, he destroyed, defaced or sold all the regalia, except for the eagle-shaped golden ampulla from which the holy oil is poured at coronations, and the annointing spoon. These, as far as is known, were secreted from him by priests at Westminster. Some of the prices Cromwell accepted were ludicrously low. The legendary Black Prince's Ruby, which is about the size of a hen's egg, went for £15.

After Charles II's restoration, a few of the old pieces were recovered, but for the most part the regalia had to be made anew. The crowns, sceptres, spurs, orb and so on that were created for his coronation form the basis of today's collection, although much has been added by succeeding monarchs. In 1870, the jewels were moved to the Wakefield Tower on the southern inner wall. There they stayed, in a handsome vaulted chamber that dates from the reign of Henry III, until 1967 – except during the two World Wars when, with other national treasures, they were taken to remote hiding places, probably caves in Wales. The tremendous increase in tourism over recent years finally made the Wakefield Tower impractical: it has a cramped staircase that couldn't cope with the crowds. Today the treasure – the crowns and diadems, swords and sceptres, salts, pattens, flagons and fonts – is beautifully if somewhat less romantically displayed on two spacious floors of the Waterloo Barracks, which were built by the Duke of Wellington.

The most magnificent object in the entire collection, and possibly the most valuable in the world, is the Imperial State Crown which was made for Victoria's coronation and has been used by every sovereign on state occasions ever since. It contains 3,250 precious gems, including four large drop pearls which Elizabeth I wore as earrings; the Black Prince's Ruby; the romance-laden Stuart Sapphire; a second sapphire that came from the ring worn by Edward the Confessor at his coronation in 1042; and the second Star of Africa, cut from the famous Cullinan Diamond and added in the twentieth century.

The Black Prince's Ruby, an ancient uncut lopsided stone which is set in the centre at the front of the crown, has the bloodiest history of all the royal jewels. It is not, in jewellers' terms, a true gem, but rather a spinel or ballas ruby, which makes it only semi-precious. It can be traced back to the fourteenth century when Pedro the Cruel of Castile took it after he had murdered the Moslem king of Granada. Then Pedro's brother usurped his throne, and Pedro entered into an alliance with the Black Prince, the eldest son of Edward III. The prince's English forces defeated the usurper at Nájera in 1367, and Pedro rewarded him with the ruby. It has been said, but never confirmed, that the Black Prince wore it thereafter in his battle helmet. It is certain,

8 Chapel of St Peter ad Vincula, Tower of London

however, that it was set in the crown that Henry V perched atop his helmet several decades later at the Battle of Agincourt. The Duc d'Alençon, attacking the king with his sword, struck the crown but missed the ruby by a fraction of an inch. The stone has been in state crowns ever since Charles II's reign.

The Stuart Sapphire has had an adventurous career of its own. No one knows how or when it came to be among the crown jewels. It may have been confiscated in the fifteenth century by Edward IV from the Archbishop of York, in reprisal for his having at one time held him prisoner. Henry VI, Henry VIII and Edward VI each wore a sapphire in his crown, which may have been this. It could have been one of two sapphires owned by the first Stuart, James I. It quite definitely appeared in the new crown made for his grandson, Charles II. When Charles died it was passed on to his brother, the Catholic James II, and when William III drove James into exile, the stone went with him – in his pocket, it has been said.

He handed it down to his son, the Old Pretender, and after the downfall of the Young Pretender, Bonnie Prince Charlie, the sapphire came into the hands of his brother, Cardinal York, who wore it in his mitre. Some accounts say that the cardinal, having at long last reconciled himself to the fact that the Stuart line was finished for ever, simply gave the stone, with other family jewels, mementoes and papers, to the Hanoverian Prince of Wales, later George IV.

The truth of the matter seems to be that the man whom the prince's unofficial envoy to the Vatican chose as messenger, an Italian named Angiolo Bonelli, had a difficult time crossing Europe. England was then at war with Napoleon, and Bonelli, carrying a packet of value to England, could have been picked up as an enemy agent. By roundabout routes he made his way to Leipzig, and there he met a Venetian merchant who showed him a large sapphire in a diamond setting which Cardinal York had sold to him, telling him that it was part of the family treasure. Those were difficult days for exiled Stuarts, and this was probably the truth. Bonelli bought it and eventually delivered it to the Prince of Wales, who repaid the sum he had given the merchant of Venice. For the first time in about a century and a quarter, the sapphire was back in English royal hands.

As king, George kept at least some of the crown jewels in his fanciful pavilion at Brighton, and often fingered and fondled the Black Prince's Ruby and the Stuart Sapphire. To his favourite mistress of the 1820s, the plump and pink Marchioness of Conyngham, he lent – or perhaps even gave – the sapphire. She was once seen wearing it as the centrepiece in 'a diamond belt three inches wide', and later it shimmered in her headdress at a ball at Devonshire House. Reluctantly, one may be sure, she was eventually persuaded to return it, probably by William IV.

It was at last emplanted in Victoria's Imperial State Crown, just below the Black Prince's Ruby, in 1837. It is now, however, at the back of the crown, and set in its former place is the Second Star of Africa. Weighing 317 carats, it is the second largest of the diamonds cut from the massive Cullinan. The pear-shaped Star itself, at 520 carats, is not only the largest cut diamond in the world but considered by experts to be the most perfect; it gleams in the head of the royal sceptre.

The stone was discovered in 1905, clinging to the wall of a De Beers diamond mine in South Africa. It looked like an ungainly chunk of crystal, but on examination proved to be history's largest diamond, tipping the beam at 3,106 carats. It was named after the De Beers company president, Mr Thomas Cullinan, who was as nonplussed as he was delighted by this monster. What could one do with it? You couldn't set it in a ring. You couldn't hang it around a woman's neck, unless she were the size of, say, the Statue of Liberty. Finally he sold it to the Transvaal government, who had decided that it would make a most acceptable gift for Edward VII's 56th birthday.

Officials merely wrapped it in brown paper and sent it off to the king by parcel post. This was less casual than it seemed. With much fanfare, a replica was locked in a safe aboard a London-bound liner to distract potential thieves.

Edward was as baffled by it as Cullinan had been, and finally concluded that if it were to be of any use in the regalia, it would have to be cut. He entrusted the delicate task to the firm of Jack and Louis Asscher in Amsterdam. We once had a chat with one of the experts who was present the day the Cullinan was split. He told us, 'The stone was placed on a work-bench and Jack Asscher picked up his hammer. We held our breaths. Millions hung upon the accuracy of a single stroke. A fractional error could ruin the diamond. The hammer came down with a sharp crack, and all was well.' The Cullinan provided not only the two enormous Stars of Africa, but two lesser Stars – 95 and 64 carats – as well as a number of smaller stones, some of which were made into a necklace and a brooch; others went to pay the Asschers for their expertise.

The two smaller Stars were placed in the crown Queen Mary wore at the coronation of her husband, George V, in 1911. But the stones you see in her crown at the Tower are only paste replicas. The real diamonds belonged to Mary personally, and she had them made into a pendant brooch which she bequeathed to Elizabeth II. The Queen refers to them as 'Granny's chips'.

When we walked into the old jewel chamber in the Wakefield Tower, builders were at work replastering and painting. Though the regalia has gone, the place is by no means empty. Here, General Raeburn showed us the block that was used for the citadel's last beheading, on 7 April, 1747. The victim was Lord Fraser of Lovat, condemned for his part in the second Jacobite uprising. There are two notches in the top of the block, showing that the headsman had needed two strokes to sever the head from the body. Leaning nearby is the axe with which he bungled the job.

On one wall in the same chamber is a deep embrasured window that recalls a far more gruesome tragedy. It was here that Henry VI, imprisoned during the Wars of the Roses, was stabbed to death as he knelt in prayer. The murder was almost certainly at the order of the future Richard III. Though Henry was far too weak both physically and mentally to survive the rigours of kingship in the violent years during which he reigned, he was, nevertheless, beloved for his goodness and holiness. He founded both Eton College and King's College, Cambridge, and every year representatives of both lay memorial tributes of lilies and roses on this bleak spot.

Connected with the Wakefield Tower by a narrow spiral staircase is the bastion originally called the Garden Tower, but redubbed, for good and gory reason in the sixteenth century, the Bloody Tower. The list of unwilling guests is enormous, some who were arch-villians, some who were guiltless – prelates and plotters; peers and princes; the infamous Jeffreys, hanging judge of the bloody assizes; Sir Walter Raleigh, and, possibly, the handsome, gullible, avaricious Duke of Monmouth, Charles II's first-born bastard, who, ever seeking the crown, was defeated at last by the forces of his uncle, James II, and executed on Tower Hill.

One prisoner, Sir Thomas Overbury, was cast into the Bloody Tower in James I's day because he opposed the marriage of a friend of his, Robert Carr (later the Earl of Somerset) to the wife of the Earl of Essex. Not only did the irate countess persuade the king to imprison Overbury, but she saw to it that he was silenced forever by inducing his attendants to poison his food with an incredible variety of hideous substances: arsenic, Spanish fly, hemlock, mercury, powdered diamonds and ground spiders. His constitution must have been made of iron; the post-mortem showed that he had ingested enough poison to kill 20 ordinary men.

The best-known of all the Bloody Tower's prisoners were the 'little princes', the 13-year-old who was about to be crowned King Edward V, and his brother, the Duke of York. The late king's brother, the Duke of Gloucester, convinced the widowed queen to let him 'protect' the young monarch in the Tower. Then he himself seized the crown and, as Richard III, had both boys done away with to prevent any threat from them to his usurpation. Or so the story goes.

Shakespeare, relying on the posthumous account of the double murder written by Sir Thomas More (and no doubt anxious to please his Tudor queen by blackening Richard's fame), gave Crookback no benefit of the doubt. More recent scholars have tried to prove him free of guilt, and to pin the crime on his successor, the first Tudor, Henry VII. Sir Winston Churchill, however, gave credence to the Shakespeare-More version. Richard, he wrote, had the three essentials for premeditated murder: opportunity, means and motive.

If this is so, here is how the crime was committed: In July, 1483, Sir James Tyrrel, a soldier and creature of Richard's, coerced the constable into turning all the keys over to him for one night. Then

Tyrrel's groom and one of the jailers guarding the princes crept into the room as they lay sleeping side by side, smothered one with a pillow and stabbed the other. They buried them hastily in the basement. The constable, aghast at the crime, had them reburied with a proper religious ceremony.

No one knew where they lay until Charles II's time, when workmen digging near the White Tower found a coffin containing two small skeletons. Charles's surgeon examined them and declared that these were the bones of the princes. The king now had them interred in the Henry VII Chapel at Westminster Abbey, with an inscription declaring them unequivocally to have been the victims of their uncle, Richard III, 'usurper of the realm'. Still they were not to rest in peace. In 1933 they were exhumed again, and experts concluded once and for all that these were indeed the remains of the innocent boys murdered 450 years earlier in the Bloody Tower.

From almost any vantage point, whether within the fortress or outside its walls, it is William's 900-year-old central keep, the White Tower, that catches the eye. Yet, though it is the oldest structure of all, it looks almost new, so firm are its lines, so clean and straight its walls. Strangely, the White Tower also appears somehow less military, less truculent, than the bastions which encircle it – almost a fantasy conceived by Tolkien and designed by Disney.

Its chief function today is to house one of the world's finest armour and weapons collections. For serious students of antique arms, or merely for the youngster who has been exposed to Malory for the first time, these whitewashed stone chambers reverberate with the clash of steel and the cry of battle. For those less combative in spirit, it is rather fun to note from two of Henry VIII's suits of armour – one dating from his youth, the other the last he wore – that his waist measurement expanded from a willowy 32 to a well-padded 52. By his day, armour was already more for display and for such events as tilting matches than for the serious business of war. Some of the most gorgeously-etched and glittering suits in the Tower were worn only for pageantry.

There is, however, also an encyclopaedic array of the more business-like side of the armourer's art, from big, clumsy two-handed claymores to elegantly slim but efficiently murderous rapiers, everything that man at his most lethal-minded ever devised – clubs, maces, flails, battle-axes, lances, spears, pikes, bills, halberds, partisans, long-bows, crossbows, javelins, cannon, mortars, muskets, shields, daggers and dirks.

The White Tower's council chamber on the top floor was the scene of one of history's most sorrowful abdications. Here, Richard II took his crown from his head and handed it to his cousin and conqueror, Henry Bolingbroke, Duke of Lancaster, who reigned as Henry IV. The Tower held mixed memories for Richard. He had taken refuge within its walls from the violent mobs during the peasant uprising led by Wat Tyler. And within its walls he had entertained extravagantly. The chronicler, Jean Froissart, described a tournament he staged 'with threescore coursers . . . and ladies of honour mounted on fair palfreys [accompanied by a] great number of trumpets and other minstrelsy. . . .' That night 'there was goodly dancing in the queen's lodging . . . and ladies and demoiselles continuing till it was day'.

Now Richard, a sometimes foolish, sometimes courageous, always pleasure-loving king, was broken and demoralized. He faced the moment 'when the kissing had to stop'. His voice must have quavered: 'I have been King of England, Duke of Aquitaine and Lord of Ireland above 22 years, which signory, royalty, sceptre, crown and heritage I clearly resign here to my cousin. . . .' Shakespeare wrote it better, but Richard's spare language is moving. He was bundled off to Pontefract Castle where he died, or, according to some historians, was slaughtered.

One floor below the council chamber is the Chapel Royal of St John the Evangelist, where the body of the murdered Henry VI lay in state; where the nine-day queen prayed before her execution; and where the Order of the Bath, the second of the great Orders of Chivalry, was founded in 1399. The candidate knights kept their vigil before the altar on the eve of their dubbing, which was also the eve of a new sovereign's coronation. In those days the knights really were bathed, in a tub in an adjoining room, and the monarch traced the sign of the cross on their bare backs.

Charles II – he was nothing if not a West End man – moved the ceremony to the Painted Chamber in Westminster Palace. But the Chapel of St John, except for some minor changes made by Sir Christopher Wren, remains substantially as it was when the Normans built it, its columns thick and squat, its arches sturdy, the curve of its apse protruding from the south-east corner of the White Tower.

The second of the Tower's two chapels, St Peter ad Vincula, was built in the eleventh century and rebuilt after a fire had destroyed it in the sixteenth. A former Tower governor, Colonel E.H. Carkeet-James, made the interesting and perceptive point that while Westminster Abbey and St Paul's Cathedral are the burial places of Britain's successes, the chapel holds only its failures. They lie in neat rows, this army whom life, sometimes cruelly and capriciously, sometimes justly, defeated. At their head before the high altar is James, Duke of Monmouth. Among those in the ranks that follow are Anne Boleyn, Catherine Howard, Lady Jane Grey and her husband, passionate Essex and poisoned Overbury. Macaulay wrote of St Peter ad Vincula, 'In truth there is no sadder spot on earth.'

The years have purged the chapel's melancholy, as they have the horror of Tower Green. Time is a merciless unromantic. On one side of the Tower's curtain walls is a new shopping centre; on the other stands a tall modern hotel below which smart yachts lie moored in a marina where once the salt-stained galleons of the Virgin Queen dropped anchor, back from the Spanish Main.

III
THREE PALACES

Young Queen Charlotte threw back the shutters in an upstairs room of her new home to reveal to George III, her husband of ten months, the surprise she had prepared to celebrate his 24th birthday and their housewarming. Stretching across the greensward below was a white semicircle of arches, spires and finials, gleaming softly in the light of thousands of glass lamps. An orchestra played, and guests promenaded beneath the arches past illuminated paintings – of the king bringing peace to the world; of Britain's military triumphs; of the evils of mankind majestically defeated. It was part *fête champêtre*, part *Midsummer Night's Dream*, an immoderate toy given by an open-hearted 18-year-old girl and devised by the most prolific and most protean architect of his time, Robert Adam.

The date was 6 June 1762, and it was the first royal occasion ever to take place in what we know as Buckingham Palace. In those days the mansion, set in gardens that faded off into parkland and empty fields to the west, was called Buckingham House. It was the newlyweds' personal town residence; St James's Palace, several hundred yards along the Mall, was their official home. George had bought Buckingham House – soon to be called Queen's House – as an eventual retreat for Charlotte in case he should die before her. But the couple quickly found that they preferred its airiness and informality to the sombre antiquity of St James's. They settled down to a life of domestic tranquillity (in marked contrast to the political storms that raged in George's reign), and in Buckingham House all but the first of their 15 children, the boy who became George IV, were born. (His birthplace was St James's.)

The seeds of the world's most renowned inhabited palace were

9 Buckingham Palace

sown – quite literally – in the seventeenth century by James I. More than 800 acres of today's central London, approximating St James's Park, Green Park, Hyde Park and Kensington Gardens, had become royal property in Henry VIII's acquisitive day. James, envious of the flourishing silk industry in France and trying to make work for the unemployed, decided to plant mulberry trees on four acres of this Crown Land, with the aim of raising silkworms. But his technical advisers were not all they might have been; instead of planting white mulberries on the leaves of which silkworms dote, his gardeners laid out black ones. The project failed and eventually all but one of the trees disappeared; it stands, marked with a plaque, at the bottom of Buckingham Palace's 40-acre private garden.

Records of the mulberry plantation after James's time are vague. By the reign of his son, Charles I, it seems to have become 'a place of refreshment'. In 1654, five years after Charles's execution, the diarist John Evelyn, wrote that the Mulberry Garden was 'now the only [rendezvous] about the town for persons of the best quality'. (Cromwell

had closed down the popular Spring Gardens across St James's Park.)
With the Restoration, it was leased out for 'publique entertainments'.
The buildings that had housed the silkworms were turned into
restaurants, and intimate nooks were erected under the trees. Charles
II used to drink and gossip with other gallants there.

The playwright, Sir George Etheridge, gave one of his characters
the line, 'There is temptation enough [in the garden] to stir up the
Courage of an Alderman.' One of Thomas Shadwell's brainchildren
commented, 'the Garden was very full . . . of gentlemen and ladies, that
made love together till twelve o'clock at night.' Pepys, who tried everything and lifted his eyebrows at nothing, did not think much of the
Garden on his first visit: '. . . a very silly place . . . and but little company, and those of a rascally, whoring, roguing sort of people, only a
wilderness, that is something pretty, but rude. Did not stay to drink.'

By then a house had already been built on half an acre adjoining,
a freehold grant from James I to the first Earl of Middlesex. The land
was eventually sold to Lord Goring, later first Earl of Norwich, an
ardent Royalist and one of Charles I's generals during the Civil War.
Goring enlarged the original building and began to negotiate for
adjacent land. He had not completed the deal by the time he died in
1663, but Goring House, standing on ground now occupied by the
northern wing of Buckingham Palace, was, in terms of splendour, a
fitting antecedent for the royal home.

The outlines of the present property began to take shape with Henry
Bennet, Earl of Arlington, one of Charles II's Cabal. He not only
managed to obtain the extra land Goring had wanted, but to get a
99-year lease from the Crown for the Mulberry Garden as well.
Influential both politically and socially, he turned Goring House into
almost a second court. Furnishings were extravagant and entertainment lavish. Then the house burned to the ground with 'hardly
anything', Evelyn noted, 'saved of the best and most princely furniture
that any subject had in England'.

Arlington rebuilt on an even nobler scale. His new Arlington House
had a chapel, a bowling green, an orangery and stables for 40 horses.
Lady Arlington ordered from Paris 'enough of the finest Venice
brocatelle to make hangings for the ante-room, and covers for 12
chairs, bed curtains in green damask, and coverings of the same stuff
for a sofa, a set of chairs, and fauteuils in another chamber.' It was
perhaps seated on one of those fauteuils that Charles II laid eyes for
the last time on his troublesome son, the Duke of Monmouth, before
he sent him into exile. The encounter took place in Arlington House.

Another of Charles's illegitimate sons, the adventurous Duke of

Grafton (this one by Lady Castlemaine), was the first person of royal blood to live where Buckingham Palace now stands; his wife was Arlington's daughter, and she inherited the house. But his tenure was brief. Within five years he was killed in battle while serving under Marlborough at Cork, and his widow abandoned London for her father's estate near Newmarket.

Arlington House was let for a time to the Duke of Devonshire, again partly destroyed by fire and sold in 1703 to John Sheffield, Duke of Buckingham. He razed what remained of Arlington's mansion and, with the permission of Queen Anne (he had once wooed her, and she had bestowed the lapsed Buckingham title on him), he lopped off a bit of St James's Park to extend his property eastward. Then he built what a contemporary newspaper prophetically described as a 'graceful palace . . . not to be contemned by the greatest monarch'. It was, however, to be more than half a century before George III, the first monarch to dwell in it, bought it for £28,000 from Buckingham's heir.

Previous sovereigns had used other London palaces for centuries. Let us look at these before returning to Buckingham Palace, whose present eminence dates only from Queen Victoria's accession in 1837.

Rulers from Henry VIII to George II had lived chiefly first in Whitehall (see Chapter IV), then in St James's and finally in Kensington Palace at the western end of Hyde Park. Henry built St James's Palace in the 1530s on the site of a hospital for 'maidens that were leprous' which had stood there since before the Norman Conquest. He was, at more or less the same time, completing Bridewell Palace near Fleet Street; enlarging Whitehall and Hampton Court; building Queen's House in the Tower, and working on a couple of additional country hideaways, Nonsuch Palace near Cheam, and Oatlands near Chertsey.

He intended St James's, it appears, as a gift for Anne Boleyn, whom he had recently married. His initial and hers – H and A – are carved over the mantel in the presence chamber and above two small doorways which flank the Holbein Gate. They could have afforded Anne little consolation when, some three years after they were incised, she laid her head on the block.

In the shadowy courtyards of St James's at twilight, with the old gas-lamps glowing on weathered brick, one ghostly figure after another whispers by. Here is Bloody Mary at her death lamenting Britain's loss of Calais. Here is Charles I saying his last prayers on the eve of his execution. Here is the 15-year-old Duke of York (later James II) hastily disguising himself in girls' clothes to escape to the Continent

10 *left* The Royal Mews, Buckingham Palace

11 *below* The State Coach, Royal Mews

and join Charles II in exile. Here is James's first wife, Anne Hyde, pondering Pilate's question as she dies, 'What is truth?' And here is the realistic Queen Caroline on her deathbed, counselling her adulterous husband, George II, to marry again. Sobbing, he said, '*Non, j'aurai des maîtresses!*' She replied, '*Ah! Mon Dieu, cela n'empêche pas.*'

George II lived on in the palace with his mistresses, as he told his wife he would. Their ghosts are there too. And in the Chapel Royal is a long procession of spectral royal brides and grooms, from William and Mary in 1677 through Victoria and Albert in 1840 to George V (then Duke of York) and Mary of Teck in 1893.

Although Charles II was born in St James's, big bustling Whitehall was far more his style, and he turned the smaller palace over to his brother James. He did, however, ensconce one of his last mistresses in St James's, the beautiful Hortense Mancini, niece of his old enemy, Cardinal Mazarin. And he, more than any other monarch, is responsible for the fashionable tone of the entire corner of London which Oscar Wilde, about two centuries later, called 'our little parish of St James's'.

The sense of intimacy, almost privacy, of St James's Park was also largely Charles's doing. It had been part swamp, part wilderness when Henry VIII built his palace, which he used chiefly as a hunting lodge. Henry drained the ground and walled it, and ensuing rulers gradually tamed it further. During the Commonwealth Mrs Oliver Cromwell's cows were let loose to graze where Charles I's deer had roamed. When Charles II regained his throne, he sent to France for Louis XIV's gardener, André Le Nôtre, who had laid out the gardens of Versailles and the Tuileries. The Frenchman did not, as he had done for the Sun King, advise formality, but suggested instead that Charles make the most of the park's natural contours, 'its rural and, in some places, its wild character'.

Le Nôtre created an aviary – hence Birdcage Walk – and linked a string of pools into a canal, where he placed a decoy for ducks and wild fowl. (Under George IV, the canal was transformed into an ornamental lake by his favourite architect, John Nash.) Evelyn recorded that 'staggs, Guinea Goats and Arabian sheepe' also wandered in the park.

Charles threw the whole thing open to the public and because he enjoyed them so much himself, its lanes and walks became the most fashionable promenades in London. He fed the ducks, strolled with his spaniels, chatted with friends and strangers alike, and played *paille-maille*, a sort of imported croquet, from which the names of both the Mall and Pall Mall derive. Even in midwinter the park was thronged. On 1 December 1662, Evelyn saw 'the strange and wonderful

12 *above* Brooks's Club, Westminster

13 *left* Boodle's Club, St James's Street

dexterity of the sliders on the new canal . . . performed before their
Majesties by divers gentlemen and others with skates, after the manner
of the Hollanders; with what a swiftness they pause, how suddenly
they stop in full career upon the ice.'

Charles installed Nell Gwyn in a house in Pall Mall, on the site of
today's Number 79. Since it was royal property, he gave her only a
leasehold, not a freehold. She returned the lease with a characteristic
comment: she had always offered her services free under the Crown and
expected the Crown to do the same for her. She got her way, and
Number 79 has been privately owned ever since, although the rest of
the street remains Crown property. Nell's garden was separated from
the park only by a low wall, and she would often call out to the king
across it, asking if he planned to stay with her that night. The censorious
Evelyn was 'heartily sorry at' the behaviour of this 'impudent comedian'.

Courtiers and privy counsellors made their homes near the park,
some in the newly developing Mayfair north of Piccadilly, and left
their names behind in streets where smart Londoners now bespeak
hats and shoes and hand-made hunting guns – Albemarle, Jermyn,
Arlington, Bennet, Bond, Burlington, Berkeley.

The world of St James's, the area between the Mall and Piccadilly,
between Green Park and the Haymarket, is probably the last bastion
of the sort of masculine elegance with which London's name is
synonymous. This is Rolls Royce territory, the land of grouse and
port and Havana cigars, of Old Masters under the hammer at Christie's
in King Street, and morning coats and toppers at the Ritz after
Buckingham Palace garden parties. Above all, it is clubland.

White's, the oldest club for gentlemen, began as a chocolate house
during the reign of William and Mary. Others developed over the
eighteenth and nineteenth centuries from coffee houses and taverns.
Today their façades, some Georgian classic, some Victorian Renaissance, testify to the wit, wisdom, shared tastes and eccentricities of
their respective memberships – Brooks's, Boodle's, the Carlton, the
Reform, the Travellers, the Athenaeum and so on.

Gilbert characterized the Athenaeum in *The Gondoliers*:

> *Ambassadors cropped up like hay,*
> *Prime Ministers and such as they*
> *Grew like asparagus in May,*
>   *Professors three a penny . . .*
> *Lord Chancellors were cheap as sprats*
> *And Bishops in their shovel hats*
> *Were plentiful as tabby cats,*
>   *In point of fact, too many.*

Almost all of seventeenth-century St James's has been whittled away by succeeding generations of architects. In Pall Mall only Schomberg House (in the eighteenth century the home of Thomas Gainsborough) remains with at least part of its original brown brick intact. And Wren's parish church still stands in Piccadilly. Badly bombed in World War II, it was reconstructed within its small serene garden, a gratifying caesura in the pounding rhythm of commercialism. At Pall Mall's western end, walled off from the street in its own grounds, is Marlborough House, which was also built by Wren – this, in 1709, for the thrusting, victorious John Churchill, first Duke of Marlborough. It remained in his family for about a century, then passed to the Crown and became a subsidiary royal residence. It was the home for 27 years of the late Queen Mary, and is now a centre for Commonwealth conferences.

Although no monarch has lived in St James's Palace since 1837, the passing of one ruler and the accession of the next is still proclaimed from its balcony in Friary Court. Foreign ambassadors are still accredited, not to Buckingham Palace, but to the Court of St James's. The lord chamberlain, who is responsible for the management of the queen's household, has his offices here. And a handful of royal relatives are always housed on the premises. The Duke of Windsor lived in York House, in Ambassadors' Court, before his brief reign as Edward VIII. York House is now the London residence of the Duke and Duchess of Kent. Queen Elizabeth, the queen mother, is around the corner, not in the palace itself, but within its ambit, in Clarence House, a roomy white mansion built by Nash for William IV when he was Duke of Clarence. It was here that the present queen, then Princess Elizabeth, and the Duke of Edinburgh made their first home.

Little of St James's is open to the public. Visitors can attend Sunday services from October until Easter in the Chapel Royal, which opens off Ambassadors' Court. They can worship between Easter and the end of July in the small, exquisite Queen's Chapel across the road from Friary Court, in the grounds of Marlborough House, Inigo Jones created it for Charles I's French Catholic queen, Henrietta Maria; Charles II's sadly neglected Catholic queen, Catherine of Braganza, also worshipped there.

After Charles's younger son, James II, was driven into exile by his own daughter, Mary, and her husband, William of Orange, royal London moved west. William suffered from asthma, and feared the river mists at Whitehall Palace. As for St James's, the couple simply

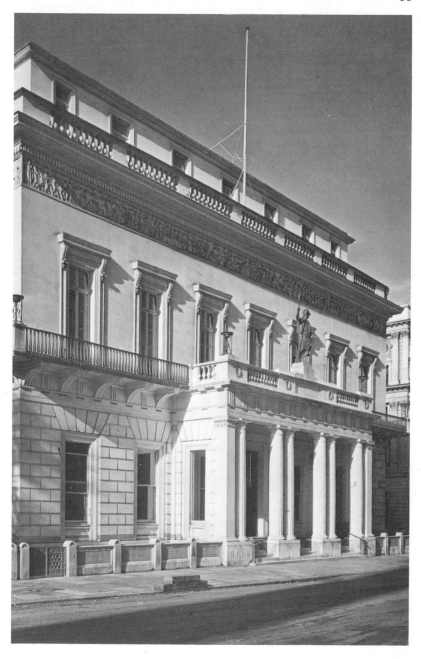

14 The Athenaeum from Waterloo Place

didn't like it. They established their court out of town, in the village of Kensington. Today traffic pounds along the High Street a few score yards from their graceful palace, and the public roam freely through its chambers. But in those days, the dwelling they chose, a house that belonged to the second Earl of Nottingham, was far out in the country. The environs were dangerous and footpads harried travellers.

When William and Mary called in Christopher Wren (what *would* London have looked like without the 'Wrenaissance'?) to modernize and enlarge Nottingham House, one of the first things he did was to lay out a straight well-lighted road eastwards through the park, the *Route du Roi*. Londoners soon called it 'Rotten Row'; the stretch that remains is now a public bridle path.

Wren clothed the walls in brick, added a clock-tower with a weather-vane, galleries and staircases, chambers for maids-of-honour, courtiers and guards, and hired Grinling Gibbons to embellish walls and mantels. Inside the King's Gallery, above the chimneypiece, was installed a wind-indicator, a long pointer which still swings – actuated by rods attached to a vane on the roof – across a painted map of north-west Europe. With sea wars a constant threat, it was essential for an island monarch always to know which way the wind was blowing.

Even though fire delayed construction, Wren managed to get the place ready within six months, a miraculous achievement when you consider that he was at the same time rebuilding Hampton Court, building the new St Paul's Cathedral and still completing some of his 53 other post-Fire City churches.

It is not impossible to imagine living in Kensington Palace. True, it contains several long passages constructed in that privacy-defying manner that seems to bedevil all palaces, where rooms open endlessly out of rooms. Admittedly, too, it has some pompous high-ceilinged chambers and a grand (though whimsically painted in *trompe-l'oeil*) staircase, all created by William Kent for George I. But most of it is on a human scale. Leigh Hunt wrote in the nineteenth century, 'Windsor Castle is a place to receive monarchs in; Buckingham Palace to see fashion in; Kensington Palace seems a place to drink tea in. . . .'

Monarchs drank tea in it for 70 years, and they all added bits and pieces to the property. Some of these were in the 200-odd acres now known as Kensington Gardens. By far the loveliest addition is the Orangery, just north of the palace. It was designed by Wren (some say with the help of Sir John Vanbrugh) for Queen Anne, James II's younger daughter. Anne was undoubtedly stodgy, and her husband Prince George of Denmark, even more so. Charles II once said that he had tried George drunk and had tried him sober and could make nothing of him either way. Yet Anne had a keen sense of beauty. Her Orangery, of red brick with white Corinthian pillars, a domed ceiling and alcoves at each end, is simple and stylish. There is no record that oranges ever grew there. Anne used it as an entertaining room: bewigged footmen served dinner while musicians played in one of the alcoves.

Nannies wheeling their prams along the Broad Walk, children and adults sailing their model boats in the Round Pond and swimming in the Serpentine, can thank Queen Anne's gardener, Henry Wise, who conceived all three – not exactly as they are today, but in principle.

Anne left no heirs, and George Louis, Elector of Hanover, was imported to succeed her, on the strength of his being both safely Protestant and a grandson of James I. He never learned to speak English and was almost totally uninterested in the country he had come to rule. This in the long run proved a good thing, because he turned political matters over to his chief minister, Sir Robert Walpole, and thus in effect established the role of prime minister. He did, however, enjoy his little palace, and he quickly set about expanding it. He needed the space: he had brought with him some 200 hangers-on, including a pair of German mistresses. He also furthered Anne's garden schemes.

But it was his son's wife, Queen Caroline of Anspach, a vigorous and altogether delightful woman, who saw the job through. Anne's plan had called for a series of ponds, fed by the old 'lost' Westbourne River. Caroline improved on this by substituting an unbroken curving lake, the Serpentine, and placing two yachts in it 'for the diversion' of the royal family. The public for the first time were also invited to use the gardens – on Saturdays, when George II's court spent the day at the lodge in the old deer park at Richmond.

Inside the palace Caroline brightened up the wood panelling with white and gilt and brought masterpieces from the other royal homes to hang on the walls. George II, however, was utterly out of tune with his wife's fastidious taste, and was furious when she substituted some excellent paintings for some execrable ones. He insisted that a 'fat Venus' to which he was partial be brought back, and that Caroline banish, in particular, 'the picture with the dirty frame . . . and the three nasty children'. This, experts have concluded, was almost certainly the Van Dyck of Charles I's children which now hangs in Windsor Castle.

With Caroline's death in 1737, Kensington Palace's high noon ended and the first long shadows of neglect fell across it. Horace Walpole,

15 *left* The organ from Whitehall, St James's, Piccadilly

16 *below* Kensington Palace with the statue of William III

author, politician, observer of the passing scene and youngest son of Robert Walpole, wrote, '. . . the King . . . has locked up half the palace . . . so he does at St James's, and I believe would put the rooms out to interest, if he could get a closet a year for them!' George II himself was dead by 1760; his son and heir had died before him, and when his grandson, George III, came to the throne he 'desired to be excused living in Kensington'.

No sovereign ever lived there again, except for the 18-year-old Queen Victoria – and that only for the first three weeks of her reign. She was awakened there between five and six in the morning on 20 June 1837, to learn from the Archbishop of Canterbury and the lord chamberlain that she was queen. Her uncle, William IV, had died a few hours earlier. So remote from the throne had Victoria's life in Kensington seemed that she had not even realized she was the heir presumptive until 1830, when her governess, Fräulein Lehzen, slipped a genealogical table into her history book.

By 18 July she was writing in her diary, '. . . It was the *last time* that I slept in this poor old Palace, as I go into Buckingham Palace today. Though I rejoice to *go* into B.P. for many reasons, it is not without a feeling of regret that I shall bid adieu *for ever* (that is to say *for ever* as a DWELLING), to this my birth-place, where I have been born and bred, and to which I am really attached. . . .'

On the day of her accession, Victoria performed one public rite and one personal one: she held her first privy council, and she moved into a room of her own. Until then she had shared her bedroom with her domineering mother, the Duchess of Kent. Her childhood room was recreated in the 1930s by Queen Mary. Filled with furniture and bibelots that either belonged to Victoria or date from her reign, it is vibrantly alive, as though the girl who lived in it had just put down her sewing and strolled out. Queen Mary had a special interest in it: she herself was born there.

Kensington Palace, after standing empty and desolate for decades, had, by the beginning of the nineteenth century, become a sort of superior dormitory for royal relatives. Two of George III's sons, the Duke of Sussex, and Victoria's father, the improvident Duke of Kent, were housed there, as were various sisters, sisters-in-law, nephews and nieces. The tradition continues. Today, the nonagenarian Princess Alice of Athlone, Victoria's last surviving grand-daughter, has a flat in the palace. So do Queen Elizabeth's sister, Princess Margaret; the queen's cousin, the Duke of Gloucester, and his Danish-born wife; and the duke's mother, the dowager duchess, Alice, widow of the queen's uncle, Prince Henry.

Buckingham Palace was not even called a palace until Victoria decreed that it should be. The famous white front facing down the Mall and the much-photographed balcony where the sovereign appears on great occasions did not yet exist. But there had been changes since George III's tenure.

His heir had a passion for building. As regent, George IV had spent a fortune remodelling Carlton House, his London home; creating that oriental extravaganza, the Brighton Pavilion, and restoring Windsor Castle. His appetite for beauty was as voracious as his love for women, wine, food and fashion. He bought furniture and *objets de vertu* from aristocratic homes in France which had been dismantled after the Revolution, and scattered them through his own residences.

When he became king he chose Buckingham House as his pied-à-terre. He did not consider it a palace, but he proceeded to make it as grand as any palace on the Continent. He was then fat, 58, and extremely unpopular. Parliament had several times had to pay off his debts, and he had been accused of wasting millions on improperly supervised building programmes. John Nash was just then completing the ambitious urban scheme which linked Regent's Park by way of the sweeping colonnaded (at the time) Regent Street with Carlton House in the Mall. In retrospect, it has been acknowledged that George's contributions, both in London and out, were architecturally important. But when he conceived them they were fiercely resented. The nation was still impoverished by the Napoleonic wars, and parliament put him on a strict budget for Buckingham House. He overspent by more than threefold.

Nash, on the king's order, retained the shell of the existing buildings. What emerged, however, was far more lavish. The wings that stretched towards St James's Park were razed and longer ones constructed in their place. There were new state rooms, bed-chambers, a picture gallery, a porticoed main entrance, a decorative stable block and an entirely new garden-front with a semi-circular bow and a broad terrace.

Marble was imported from Italy for staircases and halls. Mantels were ripped out of Carlton House and, with George's finest furniture and art, installed in the new rooms. Front and centre of the forecourt, looking eastward towards the Mall, was built a triumphal arch of white marble. It is ironic that the Arc de Triomphe, which the French were putting up at the same period to commemorate Napoleon's victories, should still stand in the Etoile where it was placed, while the arch that George built to celebrate England's victory over Napoleon, should have, within a few years, been hauled away to the corner of

Oxford Street and Park Lane, where it gives its name to one of London's most congested traffic spots, Marble Arch.

George lived long enough to see his arch placed on the site he had chosen. The palace itself, however, was not finished when he died in 1830. By then a fresh scandal had erupted over the amount of money Nash was spending. George's brother, the Duke of Clarence, who succeeded as William IV, hired a new architect, Edward Blore, to finish the job. But William grew so impatient with the money-devouring scheme that he swore he would never live there. When parliament burned down in 1834, he offered Buckingham House to the Lords and Commons. They wanted it no more than he did, and it remained untenanted until Victoria's standard was raised on top of the Marble Arch on 13 July 1837.

Victoria took her role as constitutional monarch seriously, and was determined (with some nudging from parliament) not to indulge in the sort of mindless overspending that had brought wrath down on her uncle. But that didn't discourage her from delighting in her new home. She hired an orchestra to play at dinner every night; she gave a dance every week; she took friends and relatives on conducted tours; she sang and played the piano and gambled with her ladies for modest stakes at *vingt-et-un* and whist. She used George's state rooms for concerts at which distinguished artists performed. She staged fancy-dress balls, one of which, several years after she and Albert were married, was organized to give work to the silk-weavers of Spitalfields (shades of James I and his mulberry trees). Albert came as the Plantaganet monarch, Edward III, and Victoria as his queen, Philippa. All the guests were richly robed in silken costumes of the fourteenth century.

Household management preoccupied Albert, as it was to do Prince Philip a century later. The consort rationalized overlapping jobs and cut down waste. One story has it that he found out in 1847 that 200 coloured candles were being delivered daily because someone had placed an order for that number for *one* ball nine years earlier. No one had thought to cancel until Albert summarily stopped the flow of candle wax.

By then the royal family was expanding and so, again, was the palace. Victoria had complained to her prime minister, Robert Peel, in 1845, that the four-year-old Prince of Wales, and the Princess Royal, five, could not 'possibly be kept in the nursery much longer'. She also needed more space for visiting relatives. Architect Blore went to work again, adding the present eastern block, to make the building a quad-rangle around a central court, and removing the Marble Arch. Ever since, the royal standard which shows that the monarch is in residence has flown from the roof above the central balcony, the balcony which Victoria used for the first time to watch the last Guards battalion march off to the Crimean war.

In 1854, one of Nash's protégés, Sir James Pennethorne, added a ballroom, supper room and extra kitchens. Thereafter, there were no changes until 1911, when the statue of the queen who had dominated her century, was erected on a circular plinth in front of the house she had transformed into a palace. The statue had been planned by her son, Edward VII, but was not completed until his son, George V, came to the throne. To provide a suitable background, the palace front was redesigned and refaced in Portland stone.

That Victoria sits with her back to the palace seems almost a wry historical joke. In her lifetime she had also turned her back on it. The figure facing the palace represents motherhood, and that is appropriate too. She and Albert bred nine children there, thus populating the thrones of most of Europe. But they tired of living in London, and came more and more to use Windsor Castle, Osborne House on the Isle of Wight and Balmoral Castle in Scotland. Then in 1861 Albert died. Grief-stricken, the 'Widow at Windsor', as Kipling called her, virtually retired from public life. For 40 years, until her own death, Buckingham Palace was a ghost house. She commanded that Albert's rooms be left exactly as they were when he had occupied them; on the rare occasions when she went to London, she inspected them to make certain that nothing had been moved in that strangely haunted shrine.

Edward VII, during the years his mother kept the palace shrouded, had referred to it as 'the sepulchre'. On his accession, although he was almost 60 and Queen Alexandra only three years younger, they seemed to bring a touch of youthful zest to the place. They ripped out Victorian plumbing and antiquated kitchens and soon had the state rooms alight and alive again. But Edward reigned for only nine years, and died in the palace on 6 May 1910, the first monarch to do so.

Londoners had learned only the day before that the king whom they adored was gravely ill, and they gathered in their thousands to read the bulletins which were hung on the gate. Just before midnight the final notice was posted and his mourning people walked silently away. Next morning his grandsons (later Edward VIII and George VI), the sons of the Duke of York, glanced out of their schoolroom window in Marlborough House, where the family were then living, and saw the royal standard at Buckingham Palace at half-mast. That was how they learned that Edward was dead, and that their own father

17 The Peter Pan statue, Kensington Gardens

was now the new king.

George V's wife, Queen Mary, was the great-granddaughter of Queen Charlotte, and she made it almost her life's work to gather together in the private apartments of the palace the furniture and china that Charlotte had chosen in the first place. Determinedly she tracked them down in other royal homes – wherever they had strayed – often using old paintings of palace interiors as guides to what was missing.

Her husband had a macaw he dearly loved, which used to perch on the back of his chair when he received his ministers. It seemed a harmless enough pet until a wave of hysteria swept the land because several people had died of psittacosis, or parrots' disease. Parliament rushed a bill through banning the import of parrots and all breeds related to them. This included macaws. When word reached the king he was filled with consternation. He had ordered a bride for his bird, and it was even then en route from Brazil. Certainly the monarch could not break his own law! But the minister of health had an inspiration. The newly-imposed ban was intended for private owners only; it did not include zoos, where parrots and such were kept under carefully controlled conditions. If his majesty didn't mind having the palace classified as a zoo . . .? Mind? George chuckled with delight: yes indeed, so long as no one sold tickets to 'people wanting to see the wild animals'. In Britain the temporary often becomes the permanent: Buckingham Palace is doubtless a 'zoo' to this day.

In World War I, George's household lived on the same meagre rations as everyone else. In World War II, with his son, George VI, on the throne, the palace became a symbol of national unity and resistance. The king established a shooting range in the gardens where he and his staff practised with tommy-guns, pistols and rifles. As more and more bombs fell on London, the family were at length persuaded to stay in Windsor, but King George and Queen Elizabeth drove back to town every day, to visit shattered neighbourhoods and to carry on with the interminable business of government.

The palace was bombed twice, the first time with little damage except broken windows. Three days later, while the king and queen were there, it was hit with devastating accuracy. A plane, the king recorded, came 'straight down the Mall [and] dropped 2 bombs in the forecourt, 2 in the quadrangle, 1 in the chapel [completely wrecking it] and [another] in the garden.' The queen commented, 'I'm glad we've been bombed. It makes me feel I can look the East End in the face.' On 8 May 1945 when Germany's surrender was announced, crowds cheered and waved and clung to the palace railings, calling for the king, the queen and the princesses. 'We went out 8 times altogether', George wrote.

Buckingham Palace, no matter how astringently its inhabitants have from time to time been criticized, persists as a sort of national hearthside. The British are atavistically motivated, and powerful subconscious urges draw them there on occasions both of joy and of sorrow. The doings of royalty are sometimes decried as a species of large-scale soap opera. But the comparison is shallow. Royalty in Britain, as nowhere else, is a projection of the ordinary family. Just as the nation gathers solemnly as a family for the deaths of those they loved and admired – Churchill, Lord Montgomery – so do they gather for royal events: the deaths of sovereigns, the births of princes, the marriages of princesses, and, most of all, for coronations. After Elizabeth was crowned on 2 June 1953, crowds stood in front of the palace for three nights, chanting for her and Philip to come out.

The Gold State Coach in which the queen rode from the palace to Westminster Abbey embodies the British attitude towards their sovereign. They sometimes refer respectfully, if without enthusiasm, to the 'bicycle monarchs' of northern Europe, but when it comes to their own ruler, they want old-fashioned majesty. The coach, an unbelievable vehicle in the twentieth century, expresses this. It stands in the Royal Mews, and anyone can see it. You enter from Buckingham Palace Road through a pseudo-Grecian gateway topped by a clock tower, and you are suddenly in a world of fantasy. In the cobbled courtyard liveried coachmen and footmen go about their tasks against a background of columns, arches and balconies.

The coach was made for George III and described at the time as 'the most superb and expensive of any ever built in this Kingdom'. It has been used for every coronation since George IV's. Its curlicue carvings gleam: gilded palm trees rise from lions' heads to support the roof; three cherubs, representing England, Scotland and Ireland, bear the crown on their shoulders; tritons blow conch shells to herald the approach of the Monarch of the Ocean. Framed on the sides, front and back by swirls and whorls of more gold carving are allegorical panels painted by the Florentine artist, Giovanni Battista Cipriani. For all its frothy beauty, however, the carriage is lumberingly earthbound; eight horses are needed to pull it, and even so it proceeds only at a walking pace. The rest of the queen's coaches clip along at a brisk trot.

They are all there in the mews – the Irish State Coach that she uses when she opens parliament; the Glass Coach that takes royal brides to the Abbey; all the barouches and landaus, broughams and clarences, phaetons and sociables, springy vehicles with lovely springy names, in perfect working order, in regular use for carrying foreign ambassadors when they present their credentials, carrying messengers, carrying the queen's family along the royal mile at Ascot. The horses are there too, the Windsor greys and the sleek bays, in stalls lined with turquoise tiles.

In Britain's unwritten constitution, Buckingham Palace forms an essential part of the machinery of government. After a quarter of a century on the throne, Queen Elizabeth has absorbed an encyclopaedic knowledge of public and foreign affairs. And the palace is her working headquarters, where her boxes of state papers are delivered, where she consults with her ministers, where she exercises her prerogatives to 'advise, encourage and warn'.

Entertainment too is part of the job. A state dinner for Commonwealth prime ministers may smooth the way for her own foreign and commonwealth secretary; a luncheon for leaders in various domestic fields – editors, industrialists, TV stars – broadens her own understanding of the nation over which she reigns.

About 12 times a year she holds investitures. All titles, honours and awards are bestowed in her name, from orders of chivalry – the Bath, for instance – to such lesser but still coveted honours as the CBE and MBE. Whenever possible, she bestows them personally. The ceremonies usually occur in the palace, although there was one recent exception: the queen dubbed the late Sir Francis Chichester a knight in the open air at Greenwich Palace, an echo of the dubbing of Sir Francis Drake by the first Elizabeth aboard his ship, *Golden Hind*, at Deptford.

Ordinary investitures take place in the ballroom. Some 200 recipients are invited, and they are permitted to bring two or three members of their families. The ballroom is a huge oblong chamber lighted by six chandeliers, and surrounded on three sides by triple tiers of scarlet-upholstered benches. Small gilt chairs are set out in rows on the parquet floor. To the rear is a minstrels' gallery in which a guards orchestra, in full-dress scarlet, plays palm-court music throughout the proceedings. At the opposite end on a dais stand a pair of thrones beneath a red and gold canopy.

Guests and recipients begin to arrive at ten in the morning. At eleven, a detachment of the yeomen of the guard in Tudor garb and bearing halberds, marches down the centre aisle and takes up positions on the dais. Then the queen arrives through a side door, and the musicians play the anthem. She does not occupy one of the thrones, but stands in front of them. The lord chamberlain in court dress calls out the names of those to be honoured. A gentleman usher places the appropriate decoration on a red velvet cushion; a second moves the cushion towards the queen.

Knights come first. As the prospective knight approaches, the queen is handed a light dress sword. The man kneels on the investiture stool, the queen touches him on both shoulders with the blade (this is the accolade), hangs his order around his neck and says, 'Rise, Sir So-and-so.' They exchange a few words, she congratulatory, he grateful. She shakes his hand, he bows, backs away, and the lord chamberlain intones the next name. The rate is about three a minute – knights, dames, winners of service and valour awards – for an hour and a quarter.

To investitures, guests come in their hundreds, to garden parties in their thousands. We have wandered on the lawns when there were as many as 9,000 others there. Invitation in hand, you pass through the high black and gold gates that close the world off from the palace forecourt, walk under the archway where red-coated guardsmen stamp and wheel, and into the inner courtyard. You enter by the main portico, climb a few steps into the marble hall and cross a long gallery lined with the romantic Winterhalter paintings that Victoria and Albert commissioned by the score. You walk through the vast pink Bow Room and out on to the terrace.

The scene on the lawn below suggests nothing so much as a Raoul Dufy painting. The lake, dappled in summer sunshine, curves lazily to your left. Green-striped marquees where tea is served form a perimeter, one for ordinary mortals, a second for diplomats and a third for the queen and her personal guests. Two military bands in gazebos topped with the same green-striped bunting tootle away.

The movement is fluid, ever-changing: top-hatted men in morning coats; ladies in floating summer dresses, in saris, in obis; officers in uniforms encrusted with gold braid; Africans in tribal dress; the yeoman of the guard in their scarlet and gold. Soldier, statesman, author, actor, prince of the blood, cabinet minister, tennis star – people from everywhere, waiting for precisely 4:00 p.m. when the queen and members of her family appear on the terrace and then begin to circulate through the crowd.

It is a strangely English mixture of formality and casualness. As the royals advance between wide aisles of guests, gentlemen ushers precede them. The ushers touch an elbow at random, first on one side of the aisle, then on the other. A curtsey, a bow, a smile, a moment or two of chat.

There are usually three garden parties each summer, and getting an invitation is not all that difficult. Every year the lord chamberlain's office allots a given number of invitations on a pro rata basis to all accredited organizations in Great Britain, and they distribute them as they choose. Representatives of foreign embassies are invited in alphabetical order by nation. Foreign visitors with a reasonable claim to distinction stand a good chance of getting in, if they apply to their own embassies well in advance.

You stroll around the shores of the lake, across the lawns past camellias and azaleas, along the avenue of Indian chestnut trees recently planted to screen the gardens from the skyscraper windows that now overlook them. If you're historically minded, you make a pilgrimage to the far corner of the Grosvenor Place end, to see for yourself the gnarled and spreading mulberry tree, the last of those that James I planted, where the Buckingham Palace story began.

IV
WESTMINSTER AND
WHITEHALL

WHILE the City of London was growing up in the east, a second city, Westminster, was emerging two miles to its west upon a tract of Thameside swampland. The City, soon populous, wealthy and expanding beyond its walls, held – and still holds – financial supremacy. Westminster, dominated by its Benedictine abbey, gradually became the seat of royal, ecclesiastical and governmental power. By the thirteenth century a riverside roadway, the Strand, linked the two, spawning a ribbon development of mansions and palaces. Yet, administratively, the two have always remained separate.

The City of London's boundaries are roughly as they were in medieval times, but Westminster has spread so far that today it reaches eastward to the City itself, northward beyond Regent's Park, and westward as far as Chelsea and Kensington. Its frontage along the Thames stretches for almost three and a half miles. Within this heterogeneous urban sprawl lie regions as antithetical as Soho, with its foreign restaurants and sleazy strip-clubs, and Mayfair, heartland of jewellers, bespoke tailors, Claridge's and Annabel's; the clamour of Oxford and Regent Streets and the tree-lined residential avenues of St John's Wood, Little Venice and St Marylebone; Buckingham Palace and Madame Tussaud's Waxworks.

To Londoners, however, Westminster means chiefly Parliament, the Abbey, Whitehall and 10 Downing Street. We've always thought that the worst way to look at this heart of governmental London is to be dumped down in front of the Houses of Parliament. The best way is to take a taxi to Smith Square, the centre of party political activity, and let the spirit of the region steal up on you. The best time is late in the afternoon when the tide of traffic is easing.

18 *above* Whitehall

19 *right* Georgian houses on the corner
of Lord North Street and Smith Square,
Westminster

In the middle of the square rises the Church of St John the Evangelist, nearly two and a half centuries old, bomb-gutted in World War II, gorgeously restored, de-sanctified and now one of London's least pretentious and most pleasing concert halls. The headquarters of the Labour Party are on the square's south side, those of the Conservative Party on the south-east corner, and many MPs live in the surrounding streets, well within the 'division bell' area. Yet, despite the comings and goings of politicians, Smith Square maintains an air of near-patrician aloofness; its quiet deepens as you cross to the north side, a row of early eighteenth-century houses, and enter narrow Lord North Street. This and the little streets directly to its north are among the most perfect Georgian survivals in London.

The early eighteenth century specialized in seemly terraces of three-storey (plus dormer) dwellings, with small well-proportioned rooms and modest doorways, graceful and understated. How it happened that succeeding generations left this haven untouched, even to its gas-lamps, is beyond comprehension, but not beyond gratitude. Only the house on the north-west corner of Lord North Street is 'neo', and that is discreet.

One night after a concert in St John's, we found the lamps glowing, the neat houses cheerfully lighted, the sounds of the city only a distant rumour and the pavements empty. We would have been more surprised by a motor car than by a horse-drawn carriage. And then Big Ben struck ten. As age goes in London, Big Ben is not old, but in that period setting it *seemed* old. We walked to the end of Lord North Street, zigged and zagged northward to Great College Street, then turned towards the river, making our way beside the old flint walls that conceal the Abbey's gardens and Westminster School. Ahead stretched the long pinnacled range of the Palace of Westminster. The lantern above Big Ben was alight, showing that the Commons was in session.

Today's Palace of Westminster is the third to stand here. It no longer houses royalty, as did its predecessors, but it still ranks as a royal dwelling and comes under the jurisdiction of the lord great chamberlain, one of the queen's officers of state. Theoretically, the entire palace is merely on loan to parliament by the queen who, even more theoretically, might decide to take it all back again. It now provides residences for the speaker, who has a house at the Commons end of the building, and for the lord chancellor (the speaker of the Lords), who lives in equal comfort at the peers' end. The two are separated by the long terrace that overlooks the river.

The first palace, believed to have been used by King Canute, succumbed to fire early in the eleventh century. The second began fairly unostentatiously, but grew in pomp and size over almost 800 years. It was erected in 1054 by Edward the Confessor who wanted to live close to the Abbey, then rising under his supervision. Parliament began to meet there in his reign. William the Conqueror held councils in the palace, and his son, the redheaded William Rufus, added the Great Hall. Its enormous oaken hammer-beam roof, one of the largest in the world unsupported by columns, was added by Richard II. In modern times the hall has become the setting for solemn occasions, the lying in state, for instance, of kings and statesmen. In earlier days, however, it was a kind of national crossroads, where monarchs held councils, distributed food to the poor, gave banquets and staged coronation feasts. It was also a market, with shops and bookstalls lining the walls, and at the same time, until 1882, the chief hall of justice. Sir Thomas More, Charles I and Warren Hastings were all tried there.

Pepys mentioned the hall in his diary some 400 times. He went there almost daily, to pick up gossip and to attend whatever public function was in progress. He wrote of Charles II's coronation banquet: the hall 'was very fine with hangings and scaffolds one upon another full of brave ladies. . . .' During the Great Fire he recorded that the place was filled with the salvaged possessions of Londoners, and once he saw the public hangman burn three acts which had been passed by the Commonwealth parliament, among them that for 'the trying and judging of Charles Stuart'.

From the Normans to the early Tudors Westminster Palace was the busiest place in the capital. It was thronged with people who protected, prayed for and served the king, well over 5,000 at any given time, probably a tenth of the entire combined populations of Westminster and the City. There was a treasurer, a seneschal, a cup-bearer, a carver and a seal-bearer. A staff of about 100 worked in the royal kitchens, and there were more than 100 bow-makers, arrow-makers, goldsmiths, masons, carpenters, gardeners, illuminators, trumpeters and upholsterers, plus some 4,000 pages, soldiers, archers, personal servants, courtiers and religious attendants.

That monstrous beehive was partly burned down in the sixteenth century, and completely destroyed by fire in 1834. Only the little Jewel Tower has survived. It stands in Old Palace Yard at the foot of Great College Street, usually ignored both by visitors and Londoners. Three storeys high, L-shaped, made of Kentish ragstone and surrounded on three sides by a moat filled with waterlilies, it dominates its gently rolling lawns like a placid miniature fortress. Some kindly civil servant has placed a few benches on the grass so that you can sit and meditate

20 The south end of Westminster Hall

upon the indestructibility of some of man's minor works, soothed by the reflection of this particular one in the motionless jade water.

It was built in the fourteenth century at the corner of what was then the privy garden, to contain Edward III's personal jewels and plate. In due course the monarch's garments came to be stored there as well. An inventory of the tower's contents taken when Henry VIII died suggests the attic of a wealthy eccentric: a box of chessmen, some broken; a sable skin adorned with emeralds, turquoises, rubies, diamonds and pearls; several walking sticks; a stomacher of white cloth of gold raised with gold and silver tissue, a steel mirror backed with crimson velvet, embroidered with gold damask and 'garnished with small pearls', and a doll that must have belonged to Princess Mary or to Princess Elizabeth.

The entry (with the spelling modernized) reads, 'Item, a great baby lying in a box of wood, having a gown of white cloth of silver and a kirtle of green velvet, the gown tied with small aglets of gold, and a small pair of beads of gold, and a small chain and a collar about the neck of gold.' One pictures the assessor gravely dictating these dainty details to his scrivener. What a pity that the 'great baby' has not survived!

Later on, the tower became a repository for parliamentary records, and later still, in the nineteenth century, the home of the weights and measures officials. Today its little vaulted rooms are empty, save for a few bits of medieval pottery and stonework dug up nearby, and an assortment of metal weights and linear and liquid measures.

The Houses of Parliament, although they share a single roof, are as dichotomous as an ill-matched married couple. The Lords (despite the recent invention of life members with no right to pass on their titles) is still aristocratically gold and scarlet, replete with ceremonial and, on state occasions, fanciful costumes. Despite the *Iolanthe* atmosphere, however, the peers produce some of the most cogent speeches of any legislature anywhere. Unlike the elected members of the Commons, they have no need to look over their shoulders at their constituencies. They are also far less hemmed in by party loyalties, and speak with highly individualized freedom. Lord Montague of Beaulieu, owner of one of the nation's most visited stately homes, which contains a vintage-car museum, attends regularly, but limits himself to discussions of tourism, transport and rural affairs: 'In the House of Lords we have a rather sensible tradition of talking only about what we know.'

The membership includes the entire range of peers, from barons to dukes and royal dukes. The ranking member is the Prince of Wales, with his father, Prince Philip, just behind. There is also a bench of bishops headed by the Archbishops of Canterbury and York. The advent of lady peers under the Act of 1958 was expected to exert some strain on their lordships, but the only noticeable change is that there are now loos marked 'Peeresses' as well as those marked 'Peers'.

The House of Lords is not only a legislative chamber, but also the nation's highest court of appeal, and the lord chancellor outranks all other judges. A group of legal peers, the law lords, constitute his court. When the Lords are in session the lord chancellor sits below the throne upon a puffy, four-sided, crimson-covered ottoman whose back is not at its back but in its centre. It is called the Woolsack because it is stuffed with wool, in tribute to the wool industry, which used to provide Britain's most important export.

It is from the throne in the Lords' chamber that the sovereign reads the speech at the opening of each new parliament which sets out the government's forthcoming policy. And it is in the Lords that bills receive the royal assent, though not in modern times from the monarch's own lips. The assent is always given in Norman French: '*Le Roy le veult*' (The king wills it). '*Le Roy s'avisera*' (The king will think it over) is the tactful formula for withholding assent, but once a bill has been approved by both houses, a sovereign by custom never rejects it. The last to do so was Queen Anne, in 1707. When a money bill is involved, the words are more personal, recalling days when kings often had bitter wrangles with their parliaments to obtain the money they needed, or wanted: '*Le Roy remercie ses bon sujets, accepte leur bénévolence, et ainsi le veult.*' (The king thanks his good subjects, accepts their benevolence and so wills it.)

The members of the Commons are invited into the Lords' chamber only for royal assents and the opening of each new parliament. On such occasions the marital disharmony shows itself at its most acerbic, and an intermediary is needed. He is the Gentleman Usher of the Black Rod, whose wand of office is a black rod tipped with silver, and who is sent by the lord chancellor to the Commons to 'desire' them to attend in the Lords. When the queen is present, 'desire' becomes 'command'. Black Rod strides out through the Peers' Lobby and the Peers' Corridor and into the big neutral Central Hall. From then on, he is on Commons territory, but undaunted he marches on, through the Commons Corridor and into the Commons Lobby. Just as he reaches the door to the House of Commons, the sergeant-at-arms steps forward and slams it in his face.

Black Rod raps smartly at the door three times with his wand.

21 Parliament Square and the Houses of Parliament

Inside, the sergeant-at-arms places one hand warily on his sword hilt and, like the owner of a Prohibition-time New York speakeasy, peeps through a tiny aperture. He knows it is Black Rod, but – does their Lordships' messenger come with an armed force? Is he about to overthrow the people's elected representatives? Satisfied at long last, he opens the door and Black Rod delivers the lord chancellor's message to the speaker. Then the speaker leads his flock back to the Lords, where they cluster behind the bar of the House. And here is a nice niggling little point: their lordships are seated, but the commoners have to stand.

Now what is all this about? Is it a lot of solemn if entertaining nonsense? Not at all. The whole ceremony goes back to that unhappy monarch, Charles I, who entered the Commons and tried to arrest five of its members for treasonable utterances. To his command the speaker replied that he had neither eyes to see nor ears to hear except as the House commanded him. In any case, the five, forewarned, had vanished. Ever since then no reigning king has set foot in the House of Commons and no messenger from him has been permitted to enter until he has been suitably humiliated.

The English have long memories, and nowhere longer than in Parliament. Members bow to the speaker or to his chair because in the days of old Westminster Palace, the Commons sat in St Stephen's Chapel (it occupied the space now taken by St Stephen's Hall, through which the public enter) and bowed to the altar. The distance between Labour and Conservative benches is slightly over two swords' lengths, because in fierier times members might be tempted to solve knotty debating points with cold steel, and it was a wise precaution to keep them well separated.

At the end of each day's work the cry goes up throughout the building, 'Who goes home?' because long ago the surrounding dimly-lit streets were filled with footpads, and a member needed an escort to see him safely to his bed. And at the beginning of each new Parliament the cellars are searched to make certain that no latter-day Guy Fawkes is lurking below with his kegs of gunpowder ready to blow the whole glorious apparatus of state sky-high.

The House of Commons is surrounded by galleries reserved for the press, peers, diplomats, distinguished strangers (all outsiders are 'strangers') and the general public. A half hour spent there can be both amusing and enlightening, but the mechanics of the legislature need a little elucidation. All questions and speeches are, theoretically, addressed to the speaker alone, and when a member says 'Sir' it is the speaker he means. Members' names are never used. An MP refers to a colleague of his own party as 'my honourable friend'; if his 'friend' has had a military career, he becomes 'my honourable and gallant friend', and, if a lawyer, 'my honourable and learned friend'. For a member of the opposition, 'friend' is changed to a cooler 'gentleman'. Unparliamentary language is quickly chastized by the speaker. When Churchill once declared bluntly that a statement by an 'honourable gentleman' was a lie, he was duly reproved and promptly expunged his guilt by editing 'lie' to 'terminological inexactitude'.

The venerable-looking structure which houses all these archaic goings-on has been described as 'part palace, part cathedral, part railway station and wholly suitable to its mundane functions'. It is 940 feet long, has 1,100 rooms and 100 staircases. It was built after fire roared through the old palace on 16 October 1834. The blaze began underneath the Lords when workmen fed an excess of wooden tallies (notched sticks formerly used for keeping government accounts) into a furnace too rapidly. Awestruck crowds watched for nine hours as the prime minister, Lord Melbourne, led the teams battling to stem the flames. They managed to save only Westminster Hall and the adjacent crypt of St Stephen's.

The pile that rose from the ruins was designed by Charles (later Sir Charles) Barry, with the aid of the self-willed Augustus Welby Pugin, and is conspicuously 'Gothic' in every detail, from the throne in the Lords down to the umbrella stands and inkwells.

The voice of Big Ben and the clock in its tower, of course, symbolize Westminster to most of the world. But to be strictly accurate, the name, Big Ben, applies only to the thirteen-and-a-half ton bell that rings the hours. Smaller bells chime the quarters to a melody from Handel's *Messiah*.

The clock chamber is a wondrous place, if you don't mind climbing up some 350 steps to get there. We did so by special permission. One flight up we passed parliament's 'prison', a room attached to the quarters of the sergeant-at-arms which is kept ready for unruly members. None has been confined there since 1880.

At the top of the stairs we stepped out on to a gallery that runs behind the clock's four gigantic opaque faces. The minute and hour hands are 15 feet and nine feet long respectively. The pendulum is so colossal that the bracket from which it hangs had to be strengthened from the ground up to keep it stable. On a metal collar halfway up the pendulum's length lie several old pennies and half-pennies. These, idiosyncratic as it may seem, are used to regulate the most fastidiously accurate clock on earth. Add a penny and it gains two-fifths of a second

22 *left* The Jewel Tower, Westminster

23 *below* The Banqueting House, Whitehall

per day; remove one and it loses two-fifths.

Whitehall is one of those place-names which has expanded by common usage to take in far more than it designates in strict geographical terms. The map shows it merely as a shortish, slightly curving street running between Trafalgar Square and Downing Street. From there, southward to Parliament Square, it straightens and changes its name to Parliament Street. Londoners, however, think of the entire thoroughfare as Whitehall, and go even further to include not only all of the neighbourhood, but the entire civil-service side of government as well.

If Whitehall were a tributary of the Thames instead of a paved road, it could almost make a match for the Grand Canal. Most of the public buildings that line each side merit being called *palazzi*. And indeed it was because of a palace that both street and name came into being. Early in the thirteenth century, a Plantaganet statesman, Hubert de Burgh, built himself a riverside mansion. Within a few years he sold it to the See of York as a residence for its archbishops. Over three centuries, York Place, as it was then called, spread along the banks of the Thames for nearly half a mile – from what was eventually to be New Scotland Yard nearly to Charing Cross. By the time Henry VIII ascended the throne the rambling dwelling was far more palatial than any palace he himself possessed. And the current householder, Cardinal Wolsey, as Archbishop of York and also as lord chancellor of England, ran it with regal panoply, attended by some 500 servitors. No secular prince lived more splendidly.

Incautiously the cardinal invited the king to extravagant entertainments, and soon the guest, overcome with envy, became the resident. Henry did not, of course, push Wolsey out of York Place (nor out of Hampton Court) simply because he maintained too conspicuous a profile. Far more to the point was the fact that the prelate had stubbornly opposed the King's determination to divorce Katharine of Aragon so that he could marry Anne Boleyn. Henry took over York Place in 1529, and immediately set alterations and expansions of his own in train.

A narrow roadway skirted the landward length of the dwelling, and he decided to overleap it and extend his new domain. In 1532 he bought from Westminster Abbey the open fields opposite, on the far side of which he began to build St James's Palace. At York Place he bridged the road, renamed King Street, with two turreted gateways, the King Street Gate, near what is now Downing Street, and the Holbein Gate, close to what has become Trafalgar Square. This gate (given its name afterwards, because Hans Holbein the younger was believed to have designed it, but probably did not) was a fantastic structure 'with bricks of two colours glazed, and disposed in a tesselated fashion', in which were living quarters with tall windows and a passageway that led from one side of the street to the other, where Henry had laid out a sporting pleasance – covered and open tennis courts, an octagonal cockpit, a tilt-yard and bowling greens.

For those who lived in Whitehall, he issued a strict set of rules governing behaviour. They were not to 'cast, leave or lay any manner of dishes, platters, saucers or broken meat' in the galleries, outside their doors or anywhere else. They were to be 'loving together, of good unity and accord'. Most important, they were to keep 'secret all such things as shall be done or said in the [king's bedchamber]', never to discuss 'where the King goeth, be it early or late' and to avoid all 'grudging, mumbling or talking of the King's pastime'.

There were even regulations for the making of the royal bed: 'A groom or page with a torch to stand at the bed's foot; they of the Wardrobe opening the King's stuff of the bed upon a fair sheet between the groom and the bed's foot; two yeomen of the Chamber on each side to make the bed and a gentleman usher to direct them; a yeoman with a dagger to search the straw of the bed, and then to cast the bed of down upon that; and one to tumble over it for the search thereof.' Next, they must make a cross over the bed and kiss it, 'stick up Angels about the bed', set the king's sword up at its head, light the fires and finally fetch a loaf of bread, a pot of ale and a pot of wine, 'and every man drinketh'.

Neither of Henry's first two heirs, Edward VI or Bloody Mary, lavished nearly the attention on Whitehall that he had; indeed their reigns were both too brief. Although the third, Elizabeth, preferred Greenwich, she entertained in Whitehall frequently, staged tournaments in her father's tilt-yard, stocked the library with scholarly volumes, had plays performed in the Great Hall and built a temporary Banqueting House for a marriage she never intended to solemnize – between herself and the Duc d'Alençon.

After her death in 1603, when James VI of Scotland rode southward to become James I of England, her 'temporary' hall, then 26 years old, was still standing. James called it a 'shed', used it reluctantly for masques and immediately commanded a new one. He liked that little better: 'he could scarce see because of certain pillars' and was relieved when it burned down. He now ordered Inigo Jones, who had been designing ingenious settings for his masques, to create a replacement. By then the palace had some 2,000 rooms from kitchens to galleries, halls, council chambers and courtiers' apartments.

24 Horse Guards Parade, Whitehall

Of them all, only Inigo Jones's Banqueting House remains intact. Almost everything else burned down in 1698. One of the few individual objects to be spared (and that was by good luck sired of prejudice) was an organ carved by Grinling Gibbons and heavily gilded. James II had ordered it for his second wife, Mary of Modena, but when Mary of Orange arrived, she found it far too popish and, before the fire, had given it to St James's Church in Piccadilly, where it still overlooks the nave. What was left of the palace that was not consumed by flames was later demolished, except for Wolsey's old wine cellars and parts of Henry's covered tennis courts. How merciful a stroke of luck that Jones's glorious building should have escaped! Walpole wrote that it was 'so complete in itself that it stands a model of the most pure and beautiful taste'.

Chastely proportioned in the mood of Palladio, its exterior of Portland stone (the first use in London, it is believed, of this stone which became so much the city's hallmark), it overlooks Whitehall, its pedimented windows facing across the street towards the Horse Guards.

It was from one of these windows – no documentary record exists to show which – that Charles I stepped out on to the scaffold where the axeman waited.

The Banqueting House was recently restored and redecorated, and the columns in its main salon are snowy, their gilded capitals glinting beneath lustrous chandeliers. Above is a gallery with a stone balustrade on which the monarch's subjects used to lean to watch him dine. The ceiling is an explosion of baroque colour, out of key with the simplicity of the rest, and yet infinitely satisfying – nine allegorical panels painted by Peter Paul Rubens in exchange for £3,000 and a knighthood.

It was commissioned by Charles I in 1630 to extol the virtues of his less than godlike father, who had died in 1625. In the centre panel stands King James himself, a heroic figure (magnificent, if faintly ridiculous), with one foot on the globe and the other on an eagle. Cherubs and luscious females surround him, offering a crown, an orb and wreaths. In other panels, Bounty defeats Avarice, Hercules conquers Envy, Minerva stabs Lust and Government defeats Rebellion. Particularly ironic, this last!

Charles I, probably the most avid and knowledgeable art collector ever to rule England, left a Whitehall Palace filled with masterpieces. Of paintings alone there were 460, including 28 Titians, nine Raphaels and an assortment by such other geniuses as Holbein, Correggio and Rubens. When Charles II returned from exile in 1660, he found the palace gutted of beauty.

Cromwell himself had lived there, puritanically and, no doubt, self-consciously. He was not, however, as were some of his colleagues, a despoiler of royal possessions merely for the joy of despoiling. Yet he did permit many of the great works to go abroad – sold to princes of church and state who, having wept crocodile tears over the loss of Charles's head, were eager to get their hands on his goods. Gradually, after the Restoration, some of these began to trickle back. Mrs Cromwell was persuaded to part with 17 cartloads of valuables. Charles II discovered the Raphael cartoons (now in the Victoria and Albert Museum) crated in deal boxes in the Banqueting House, where Cromwell, who had bought them for himself, had stored them.

The second Charles may not have beautified Whitehall with the same zeal as did the first, but he had a lot more fun in the old place, with balls, masques, plays, spaniels, intrigues, mistresses. His own rooms overlooked the Thames, and included a privy chamber where he kept numerous clocks which had a way of chiming out of time with each other. Daily he made his way among the crowds of favour-seekers in the long Stone Gallery, his six feet two inches towering above them, listening to their problems, genuinely helping when he could, kindly and witty.

He had a laboratory built in the palace, conducted scientific experiments and encouraged men of vision to step from the age of superstition into the age of reason. But at the same time (as if to be on the safe side), he also resumed the old mumbo-jumbo of touching for the King's Evil.

Whenever he was free he crossed King Street to feed his ducks in the park or to play at tennis or *paille-maille*. Barbara Castlemaine, the incomparable nymphomaniac with the finest profile and the worst temper in London, who bore him four children, was ensconced in stylish chambers over the Holbein Gate. Louise de Kéroualle, the Breton girl and spy of Louis XIV, who bore him one son, lived in lavishly decorated apartments within the palace itself. His barren queen, Catherine of Braganza, occupied far simpler rooms. And Nell Gwyn, mother of two more of his children, of course, had her Pall Mall house.

Charles died in the palace he loved with a humble apology to his neglected wife, a jest on his lips about taking 'such an unconsionable time a-dying' and his famous injunction to his brother James not to let poor Nelly starve. When the bells tolled, all London (except for a few diehard Puritans) wept.

James II, knowing that his Catholicism must sooner or later force him off the throne, carried on for three years in Whitehall, embellishing it with carvings by Grinling Gibbons, and staving off absurd attempts by the Duke of Monmouth to unseat him. Finally, within the palace, he sentenced Monmouth to be beheaded. But staving off the threat posed by his daughter Mary and her husband, William of Orange, proved impossible.

He erected a weathervane atop the Banqueting House and watched it anxiously. If the wind blew from the east, 'the Protestant wind', he worried that it would swell William's sails for a voyage of invasion. At last came the eastern gust, and James fled, only to be captured by the usurper. After a brief imprisonment in Whitehall Palace, he was permitted to 'escape'. If you stand on the west side of Whitehall and look up at the Banqueting House, you'll see poor James's weathervane, still marking the fickle winds.

The most renowned street in all Whitehall is named for one of Charles II's most bizarre subjects, George Downing, diplomat, turncoat and property developer. An English-born Puritan, he was as a child taken to Massachusetts, where his uncle, John Winthrop, was governor. He returned home after Cromwell seized power, became a preacher with the New Model Army and then ambassador to the Netherlands, where he was as well Cromwell's chief spy on the Continent. No Englishman was better placed for assessing the temper of the times. As soon as it became clear that Restoration was inevitable, Downing embraced royalism and now spied on his one-time employers for Charles. He was rewarded with a knighthood and a Crown lease on a parcel of land abutting Henry VIII's old tennis courts and stretching between King Street and St James's Park. Here he built a string of houses, a shrewd investment, and long after his death, two of them, joined together, became one of the world's least ostentatious historic buildings, Number Ten Downing Street. Number Eleven, next door, houses the chancellor of the exchequer.

There are only two dwellings in London before which a crowd always stands, waiting for a glimpse of a famous face. One is Buckingham Palace and the other is Number Ten. The onlookers are frequently rewarded. At the palace they may well see the queen, Prince Philip or Prince Charles coming in or going out. At Number Ten they have an even better chance of a close-up of the prime minister or one of his cabinet, for Downing Street is narrow and only a few yards separate the pavement opposite from the much-photographed black door with its lion-shaped brass knocker and its hanging lantern.

Number Ten became the prime minister's home in 1735 when the first premier, Robert Walpole, accepted it from George II not merely as a home for himself, as the king had suggested, but for all future heads of government. In the eighteenth and nineteenth centuries, prime ministers did not always live there; many had more commodious London homes of their own. But almost all have used the house for business of state. In recent years it has been reconstructed to allow for a prime-ministerial apartment of eight rooms, which at least goes some way towards separating the tenant's business life from his private affairs. Even so, Harold Wilson, who often spoke of the inconvenience of 'living over the shop', preferred to reside in his own home, then in Lord North Street, when he was returned to office in 1974.

Number Ten, as you see it from Downing Street, looks considerably smaller than it is. Concealed behind its narrow façade are more than 60 rooms: on the street floor, the cabinet room, ante-rooms and offices for some 60 civil servants; one floor up, the state rooms where official receptions and banquets are held; above these, the private quarters.

The cabinet room, whose windows look out on private gardens stocked with laburnums, limes, almond trees and a lone magnolia, is distinguished though not overawing. It is 50 feet long and 20 wide, decorated in the neo-classic manner of the eighteenth century. Deep bookshelves filled with the blue volumes of Hansard's parliamentary debates line the walls to either side of a grey marble fireplace over which hangs a portrait of Robert Walpole. The long, coffin-shaped cabinet table is covered in green baize and surrounded by spoon-backed chairs. Only the premier's has arms. He sits with his back to the fireplace, a scrambler phone within reach. At each place is a blotter bound in green leather, a stationery rack filled with heavy cream paper, a pen stand, a water glass and a carafe.

In this room the destinies of a quarter of the human race have been shaped. Here Lord North, guiding England's bankrupt American policy during the War of Independence, heard of the British defeat at Yorktown and fell into a chair groaning, 'Oh God, it is all over.' Here Disraeli decided on the purchase of the Khedive's shares in the Suez Canal and sent his secretary around to Rothschild to borrow the money. It was here that the foreign secretary, Lord Grey, at the start of World War I, made his prescient remark: 'The lamps are going out all over Europe; we shall not see them lit again in our lifetime.' Here Chamberlain announced his 'peace with honour' pact with Hitler after Munich, and from here, Churchill led embattled Britain in the war that followed.

In Number Ten, domesticity and national concerns constantly overlap. The motor car of a visiting head of state may be held up by the butcher's van. The foreign secretary going out may bump into the prime minister's wife coming back from shopping. A man who spent ten years in Downing Street as private secretary to five consecutive prime ministers, once said to us, 'You might say that it's a gentleman's home in which a little government takes place from time to time.'

A pathway leads along the side of Number Ten, at the end of which is a barred gate that opens into a tunnel called Treasury Passage; this in turn cuts through to the Horse Guards Parade. To one side is a short stretch of brick wall pierced by several Tudor windows, the last remaining fragment of Henry VIII's tennis court; it was uncovered during a rebuilding programme in 1951.

From the Treasury northwards, Whitehall takes on a military air, with the new Ministry of Defence and the old War Office on the river side of the street, and the Horse Guards, a diminutive masterpiece by William Kent, and the Admiralty both on the Downing Street side.

At the Horse Guards, two mounted cavalrymen as still as statues – sometimes from the Life Guards (in red), sometimes from the Royal Horse Guards (in blue) – flank the entrance to a courtyard beyond which a deep arch leads to the broad dusty parade. This was once the tilt-yard. Every year on the sovereign's official birthday, the Colour – the standard of the foot regiment mounting guard that day – is trooped here in a blaze of dress uniforms, marching bands and wheeling soldiers. The queen, the focus of it all, rides side-saddle – small, trim, and immensely regal in military jacket and cockaded hat.

Official Westminster peters out at the north end of Whitehall in a surprisingly shabby little string of shops and pubs. Near the corner, incongruously cheek by jowl with the Admiralty, is the Whitehall Theatre which for years housed a series of phenomenally successful farces. Farce is still its *raison d'être*, but the seventies saw a joky eroticism added, with nudes and semi-nudes scampering about among the comics. It is easy to raise a disapproving eyebrow at the Whitehall Theatre (although Charles II would probably have loved it), but it is a bit less out of place than at first glance it might seem. After all, only Trafalgar Square separates the civil servants from St Martin's Lane and theatreland, and so the Whitehall is merely a harbinger.

In any case, solemnity benefits from a little light relief. Once in St Peter's in Rome, we followed our noses to the source of what seemed to be – but couldn't possibly be, we told ourselves – the rich aroma of espresso coffee. Behind a dark wooden door we found a well-stocked bar filled with priests and Vatican functionaries. If the Pope sees nothing wrong with drinkers only a few yards from his high altar, what's so shocking about nudes in Whitehall?

V
THE ABBEY

THE STRANGEST thing about Westminster Abbey is that it is there at all. When Henry VIII defied the pope, he despoiled the Abbey of many of its treasures. But although he dissolved the Benedictine monastery whose church it was, he did not level the building itself, nor the monastic quarters within its precincts, as he did with most of the other English abbeys. What then was so special about this one that caused him to stay his hand?

The answer lies in a vow made by the builder of the first Abbey, Edward the Confessor, who, while he was in exile in Normandy, pledged that if he ever became king he would undertake a pilgrimage to Rome. When he reached the throne, however, his council objected, and the pope released him from his vow, on condition that he create a monastery in honour of St Peter. So, on a site known as Thorney Island, where a thicket of thorns rose from the Thameside marsh near his new palace of Westminster, he began his promised shrine, building in the Norman style which he had come to admire in France. There is strong evidence to show that there had been a Saxon church on the spot as early as the seventh century.

Edward's monastery was consecrated on 28 December 1065, but he was too ill to attend. He died a few days later and was buried in the church he founded. The funeral procession is depicted in the Bayeux tapestry.

But the Abbey was not yet the coronation church. Edward's successor, Harold II, was crowned at St Paul's. It was Harold's conqueror, William of Normandy, anxious perhaps to associate himself with the beloved and devout Edward, who first chose to take his kingly oaths in the Abbey – on Christmas Day, 1066. Every succeeding sovereign save two (Edward V, who was murdered at the Tower before his coronation, and Edward VIII, who abdicated before he could be crowned) has done the same. Quite a parade by the time of the dissolution! What is more, the Confessor had been canonized in 1161, and later monarchs, drawn by the mystic power of his sanctity, had also chosen to be buried in the Abbey. Eight of Henry VIII's predecessors, including his own father, lay there. A mass royal exhumation would have been too much, even for him.

This royal connection, which differentiates the Abbey from all other churches, undoubtedly preserved it from Henry's wrath. There was, however, a second, almost technical reason. At the time of the Confessor's canonization, the abbot of Westminster was made a bishop and the Abbey itself came under the direct control of the pope and not that of the diocese of which it was geographically a part. When Henry overthrew Romanism in England he became, as Defender of the Faith, a sort of English pope himself. Therefore, the Roman pope's Abbey became the 'English pope's' Abbey, the abbot was transformed into a dean and some of the monks became canons. To this day Westminster Abbey – officially the Collegiate Church of St Peter – is controlled neither by bishop nor by archbishop. Its master is the dean, and he is answerable only to the sovereign. So sweeping is his authority that even the children of the sovereign must have his permission to marry in the Abbey, as must the priest who will officiate, even if it is the Archbishop of Canterbury.

The structure which Henry preserved was no longer the Confessor's church. That had been razed, not out of hatred, but out of love. Henry III, who came to the throne in 1216 as a boy of nine and reigned for 56 years, venerated the Confessor with a devotion verging on passion, and dedicated himself to erecting a church that would be a worthy resting place. He made it his life's work, and spent a fortune – his own and his subjects'. He gradually demolished the Norman building (not a stone remains above ground) and replaced it with a new one in the soaring style recently introduced for cathedrals in France. Within 24 years the entire eastern section – Chapter House, transepts, cloisters – was finished.

But there were several centuries' work to come before the Abbey, as we see it today, was completed. It was not until the eighteenth century that the two distinctive towers at the western end were constructed. The most glorious addition by far, however, was the chapel which Henry VII built – partly to honour the Virgin, partly in memory of his uncle, Henry VI, and partly to provide a suitable burial place for himself and his queen. He had the then existing Lady Chapel

25 The cloisters, Westminster Abbey

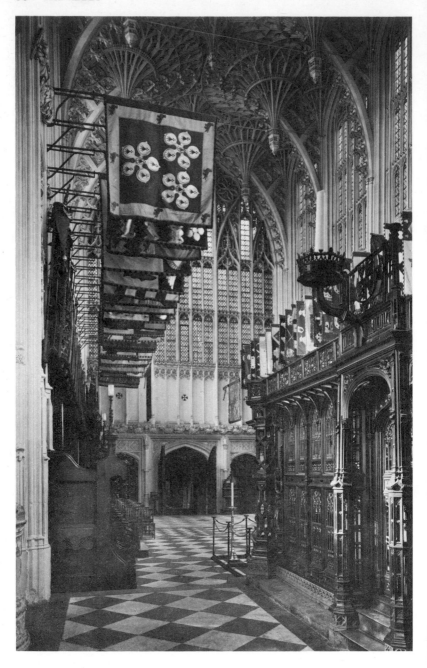

26 The Abbey: Henry VII's Chapel facing west

behind the Confessor's tomb torn down, and extended the apse to contain the fan-vaulted interior which has been called 'the most beautiful chapel in all Christendom'.

Until then, royal tombs (those at least which were in London) had been confined to the Confessor's chapel – five kings and six queens on the periphery, the saint in the centre. The Confessor's shrine, as Henry III had created it, was eye-catching and extravagant, a mass of sheet-gold and precious stones protected by golden figures of kings, saints and angels. All this, however, looked far too popish to Henry VIII who stripped it of its adornments and left it sad and dour. Even despoiled, however, it remained a place of pilgrimage, as it had been from the start. Sick people used to huddle overnight in the alcoves in the hope of a miraculous cure, and the stone steps leading to it were worn into smooth hollows by the knees of worshippers.

The Abbey is still a place of pilgrimage, but by no means for the devout alone. Some five million visitors a year make it, without a doubt, London's number one 'sight'. Why do so many people come? Only a tiny percentage who wander among the vast pillars are there to pray; even fewer are amateurs of architecture, fewer still, theological scholars. One can be certain this is so by reading a little printed sign outside the west doors which politely requests visitors, in several languages, not to 'import' iced lollies inside. What sort of people, you may well ask, are likely to import iced lollies into Westminster Abbey? The answer, quite clearly, is people who are healthily irreverent and wholly unselfconscious. Since those descriptions apply to much of the human race, it is apparent that the Abbey's appeal lies largely in its human associations – royal marriages, coronations and its pantheon-like quality as the last resting place of so many headline-making worthies.

Westminster Abbey, like it or not, is up to its flying buttresses in show business. And what a cast!

Although to most people this venerable church is the very navel of Anglicanism, there are beneath its paving-stones non-conformists, Catholics (post- as well as pre-dissolution) and even humanists. 'The rule', a former dean told us, 'is national eminence, not religious spirituality.' Ernest Bevin, the trade-unionist and wartime foreign secretary, lies in the nave, although he was a non-believer. Gilbert Murray, the Greek scholar, a Roman Catholic, also lies there, and so does Charles Darwin, the champion of evolution, whose *Origin of Species* made such a sad hash of Genesis. The British Unknown Warrior buried after World War I – symbolically, to represent the three great Allies, in a coffin of English oak, with a handful of French soil atop it, under

27 *above left* The Abbey: Poets' Corner
28 *above right* The Abbey: Coronation Chair

a slab of Belgian marble – may have been of any denomination, or of none.

The problem these days is not theology but burial space. So tightly packed are the distinguished that for many years only ashes, not bodies, have been interred. Ben Jonson may have had a prescient notion when he was buried, by his own wish, upright. 'Two feet by two is all I shall want', he told the dean. And the dean replied, 'You shall have it.'

The Poets' Corner is rather a misnomer. Not all the poets lie in the corner, nor are all in the corner poets. The literary *campo santo* began by accident. Geoffrey Chaucer, indigent in the last years of his life, had become the Abbey's clerk of works, and, as a faithful servant, was buried in the Abbey – for no particular reason, in the south transept. By Tudor times critics had begun to honour him as 'the father of the English language', so, when the Elizabethan poet, Edmund Spenser, died, the dean chose to lay the second genius beside the first. Thereafter, other literary lights began to cluster round, Chaucer and Spenser having, as it were, improved the neighbourhood.

The earlier defuncts were far more grandiloquently memorialized than those of later times. Thomas Shadwell, the dramatist, who, Dryden wrote, 'never deviates into sense', has a very showy monument. But Dickens, Kipling, Hardy and Browning rest under simple slabs. Well, *si monumentum requiris*, go to the nearest library.

Some oddities gatecrashed the Poets' Corner. Thomas Parr's sole claim to fame was his age, 152 years. Sir Richard Coxe lies there, who was taster to Elizabeth I, and so does Thomas Chiffinch, who used to lead lightsome ladies up secret staircases to Charles II's bedchamber. But John Gay, who wrote *The Beggar's Opera*, is certainly there on merit. He scribbled his own epitaph:

> Life is a jest and all things show it,
> I thought so once, and now I know it.

That is not the Abbey's only brush with humour. Once, during the reign of Richard I, it must have rocked with laughter. In those days the Archbishops of York and Canterbury were in bitter rivalry over who took precedence. The papal legate was called in to decide. Canterbury was placed at the legate's right and York offered a seat to his left. But York was not the man to be downgraded, especially before the decision had even been made. He therefore seated himself not on the legate's left – but on his lap! Canterbury's supporters pulled him off and there was a scuffle. The outcome was a typically English compromise: York was henceforth to be entitled Primate of England, but Canterbury became Primate of *All* England. And so it has been ever since.

There are over 3,300 graves plus some 400 monuments in the Abbey – a roll-call of some of the mightiest figures Britain has produced or nurtured: both the elder and the younger Pitt, Dryden, Isaac Newton, Handel, Herschel, Livingstone, Purcell, Wilberforce, Garrick, Henry Irving. Yet the muster is far from complete. Both Wellington and Nelson are in St Paul's; Shakespeare is at Stratford, Disraeli at Hughenden and Churchill near Blenheim.

Royal ladies apart, the Abbey is rather short of famous women. Among the few is Dame Sybil Thorndike, whose ashes were buried in the south aisle in July, 1976, to a fanfare of trumpets and with the psalm read by Sir Ralph Richardson, an address by Sir John Gielgud and the spell from *Cymbeline* read by Paul Scofield. Another lady, whose talents were of quite a different sort, has lain in the Abbey for almost three centuries. She was 'La Belle Stuart', Duchess of Richmond, who sat for Britannia on the old coins (she was on the penny until decimalization a few years ago) and was probably the only female whom Charles II wanted to sleep with but never did. There was, Pepys tells us, talk of forming a committee for 'the getting of Mistress Stuart for the king' and a group of noblemen actually tried to tipsify her so that Charles could make headway. But it all came to nothing, and although she and the Black Boy now lie beneath a single roof, they remain as firmly separated in death as 'La Belle Stuart' insisted that they should be when they were alive. Both are in the Henry VII Chapel, but she in the apse with her husband and he in the south aisle.

Rather ungallantly the Abbey has placed other distinguished women outside in the cloisters. Mrs Bracegirdle and Mrs Cibber, the actresses, are there, as is Aphra Behn, the first woman dramatist in English history.

The Abbey suffered many more indignities and of an even more brutish nature during the Commonwealth than it had in Henry VIII's reign. Silver was melted down, the priests' copes sold and soldiers quartered inside. They burned the altar-rail, pawned the organ pipes for liquor and used the altar itself as a mess-table. With the Restoration, steps were taken to set things right. Some tombs were in a parlous state. Henry V's beautiful queen, Katherine de Valois, lay in an open coffin of loose boards, and Pepys wrote in 1669, 'I had the upper part of her body in my hands, and I did kiss her mouth, reflecting upon it that I did kiss a queen, and that this was my birthday, 36 years old, that I did first kiss a queen.'

There was a lot still undone when James II was crowned 16 years later. So neglected was the Confessor's shrine that as the scaffolding which had been erected for the coronation was being taken down one of the choristers noticed a hole in the tomb itself. He reached inside and withdrew a golden cross and a crucifix. Then he peeped in: 'I drew the head to the hole and viewed it, being very round and firm, with the upper and nether jaws whole and full of teeth, with a list of gold above an inch broad in the nature of a Coronet, surrounding the temples.' When James was told, he had the ruinous coffin enclosed in a stout wooden case held together by iron bands.

Just in front of the Confessor's tomb stands the Coronation Chair. It was made at the order of Henry III's son, Edward I – 'Longshanks' or 'the Hammer of the Scots' – to contain the Stone of Scone, which he had filched from the Scots. It is said to be the stone upon which Jacob rested his head at Bethel. Whether it is or not, there has always been a yearning north of the border to get it back; in recent years a group of Scottish Nationalists filched it back. Eventually they were persuaded to return to Westminster Abbey.

The old oaken chair has been used in every coronation since Edward II's in 1302. Only one sovereign was not seated upon it, and that was Mary II who, being half of the only double-byline reign in English history, had to have her own chair made; her husband, William III, was using Edward's original. So great is the chair's prestige that, although Oliver Cromwell had no qualms about having the royal regalia taken from the Abbey, broken up and the jewels and plate sold for a pittance, and although he referred to the mace in parliament as a bauble, he ordered the chair moved to Westminster Hall for his own installation as Lord Protector. That was the only time it has ever been taken out of the Abbey.

Cromwell had another unique relationship with the Abbey. He and several of his Commonwealth colleagues are the only people ever to have been *un*buried from it. The Protector was entombed in the Henry VII Chapel. But a little over two years later, on the anniversary of Charles I's execution, his corpse, with those of General Henry Ireton and John Bradshaw, was dragged out, hanged on the gallows at Tyburn, their heads being afterwards displayed on stakes on top of Westminster Hall.

From time to time some extraordinarily gifted master builder so combines his materials and his inspiration as to strike a note which is completely and deeply satisfying. This happened with the Henry VII Chapel. It has an architectural kinship with the Chapel of St George at Windsor Castle, and the same forgotten genius – or geniuses – may have been involved.

Architecture is almost impossible to describe. As with music, one usually falls back on the craft's own jargon, which tends to communicate little of the sheer rapture engendered. In describing this chapel, however, even the learned Sir Nikolaus Pevsner, whose style tends to be more painstaking than poetic, departs from the language of the technician. 'A complex and triumphant symphony', says Sir Nikolaus, as his eye roams from arch to spandrel, from spandrel to fan vault. The chancel's end, he concludes, 'defeats description'.

Less defeated was Washington Irving, the creator of Rip Van Winkle: 'On entering, the eye is astonished by the pomp of the architecture and the elaborate beauty of sculptured detail. The very walls are wrought into universal ornament, incrusted with tracery, and scooped into niches crowded with the statues of saints and martyrs. Stone seems, by the cunning labour of the chisel, to have been robbed of its weight and density, suspended aloft as if by magic, and the fretted roof achieved with the wonderful minuteness and airy security of a cobweb.'

Nowadays we take it for granted that royal weddings as well as coronations occur in the Abbey. Yet the modern tradition dates back only to 1919, when Queen Victoria's grand-daughter, Princess Patricia married Commander (later Admiral) Alexander Ramsay. The magnificence of the medieval setting is said to have impressed the late Queen Mary so much that she insisted that the wedding of her daughter, Mary, the Princess Royal, to the Viscount Lascelles also take place there. Princess Mary was popular, crowds lined the streets, the lord chamberlain allotted each guest only 16 inches of sitting-space and the world press flocked to the festivities. Fourteen months later, the Duke of York (afterwards George VI) was wed to Lady Elizabeth Bowes-Lyon before the same high altar, and in 1934, his brother, the Duke of Kent, followed suit in his marriage to Princess Marina of Greece. Every important royal wedding since has been solemnized there, except that of the present Duke of Kent who was married in his bride's home cathedral, York Minster.

Television cameras invaded the Abbey for the first time during the coronation of Queen Elizabeth II on 2 June 1953. Princess Margaret's wedding to Antony Armstrong-Jones was the second case of full TV exposure. The small screen is a mixed blessing for the dean. Although it has made Westminster Abbey, with St Peter's in Rome, one of the two best-known shrines in the world, it poses grave practical problems. Not a light, not a camera, not a microphone of the 20 tons or so of equipment needed can be set in place without the concurrence of the surveyor of the fabric. Royal weddings, now seen globally, provoke a predictable reaction: for weeks afterwards the number of visitors increases to thousands above the normal.

Private Abbey weddings are rare – on average only two a year. Few people are eligible and the rules are strictly observed. If the groom, or the father of the groom or of the bride, is a Knight of the Bath, the Henry VII Chapel is made available. Peers are admissible (with express permission, of course) because the Abbey is the official church of the House of Lords. But members of the Commons must content themselves with their own little church, St Margaret's, next door. People who, like Chaucer, live in the Abbey precincts are also welcome, but usually only in St Faith's Chapel, behind the Poets' Corner.

Westminster Abbey is a victim of its own fame. So crowded is it almost always that it is difficult to concentrate peacefully on what the place really means and why Kipling wrote, 'the Abbey makes us "we"'.

For truth to tell, the 'we' is now worldwide and sometimes cacopho-
nously polyglot.

We came closest to the original intent one New Year's Eve when we
attended a watch-night service. Except for a few hundred worshippers
the vast temple was empty. It was easier then – far easier than on an
ordinary day – to picture the original abbot and his monks, corded
and cowled, telling their beads and chanting their orisons, shuffling
through the straw spread over the cold paving stones, their faces
candle-lit, their eyes downcast. When the service ended we walked
through the shadowy cloisters. Snow was falling softly and the Black
Monks of the West Monasterium came alive as they trod their daily
rounds, from cell to refectory to Chapter House to choir, confessing,
mortifying their cold flesh. Afterwards, among the New Year's
revellers it was all gone, faded, dead. *Ite missa est.*

But in the silence of the Chapter House which opens off the cloisters
– part of Henry III's original building-work – you can, even on a
bright summer's day, still sense the presence of the monks. In this
octagonal chamber they met daily with the abbot to discuss the tasks
that lay ahead. They used it, however, only for some 40 years. Then
it became the meeting house of the Great Council (for whom Henry
had possibly planned it in the first place), the body from which
Parliament evolved. And there the legislators continued to meet until
they moved to St Stephen's Chapel in the palace of Westminster in
the sixteenth century.

It was a peaceful place, the old monastery, and some of the peace
still lingers, a monument to human experience, with its layers of
memory superimposed one upon the other, as Norman crypt rests
upon Saxon fragment and Gothic arch upon Norman crypt.

Yet so enormous is the Abbey's sweep of secular history that visitors
tend to forget that it is primarily a house of worship. The dean
reminds them, albeit subtly and gently, by handing out printed copies
of a brief prayer which each sightseer is invited to repeat quietly to
himself. The words are a model of theological tact:

'O God of all the nations of the earth, Father of our Lord Jesus
Christ, and my God and Father, I believe in Thee and in Thy love to
all men and to me. In this Abbey Church of Westminster I pray,
trusting in the help of Thy Holy Spirit, for the Church of England,
for all the churches of God, for all Christians, for all who are of other
faiths, for all men. . . . Amen.'

VI
HOUSES LARGER
THAN LIFE

ROYAL palaces and high-rise blocks of flats apart, London's dwellings are on a human scale. Even a peer, no matter how time-honoured his title, may content himself when in town with a mere pied-à-terre. But it was not always so, and within the confines of Greater London are some of the grandest homes man has ever devised to slake his ego and to stagger his neighbours. We have picked out only five, four on the outskirts and one in the West End. All are open to the public.

Be it ever so sumptuous, there is, surprisingly, no place like a stately home for human-scale living. Almost all were built on a practical two-tier system, the private apartments for comfort, and the state rooms for – well, stateliness. The modern visitor sees only the latter and comes away with the erroneous assumption that the family must have spent all their time dining beneath 30-foot ceilings or passing the evening over games of chess in galleries longer than bowling alleys. He must also conclude that the possessors of these homes suffered grievously from claustrophobia.

Not long ago we dawdled away a delightful afternoon at Syon House, the London seat of the Dukes of Northumberland, whose estate stretches along the Thames in Isleworth, opposite Kew Gardens and Richmond Park. The house was closed to tourists that day, and one of the duke's staff showed us not only the state rooms, but the private apartments as well. The formal rooms might, save for the style of decoration, be part of the Louvre or the Vatican. But you could see the like of those the family use in many a well-to-do town flat.

We shall return to the interior of Syon House shortly, but first we'd like to answer a perfectly reasonable question: how and why was this vast dwelling built in the first place? Shakespeare gave us an historical

answer when he put into the mouth of Henry V these words, spoken on the eve of Agincourt:

O God of battles! steel my soldiers' hearts . . .
O! not to-day, think not upon the fault
My father made in compassing the crown.
I Richard's body have interr'd anew,
And on it have bestow'd more contrite tears
Then from it issu'd forced drops of blood.
Five hundred poor I have in yearly pay,
Who twice a day their wither'd hands hold up
Toward heaven, to pardon blood; and I have built
Two chantries, where the sad and solemn priests
Sing still for Richard's soul. . . .

Henry's father, Bolingbroke, had swept Richard II from the throne, and Richard died as his prisoner. Now, in the son's reign, conscience had assailed him for the father's sin. One of the amends he made was to establish a monastery of the order of St Bridget, the Swedish mystic, which he endowed with the income from 'the messuage, land, meadow, wood, pasture and rent, in Istelworth, Twykenham, Worton and Heston, with their appurtenances aforesaid, in free and perpetual alms forever.'

That first abbey was in Twickenham, but in 1431 the order moved to more spacious quarters; it is on the second site that Syon House stands. In its basement we saw a vaulted room filled with unwanted furniture and bric-à-brac – the original chapel of the Bridgettines, almost all that remains of King Henry's penitence.

The abbey survived until Henry VIII's break with Rome, when the king's secretary, Thomas Cromwell, passed on a report 'certefyinge the Incontynensye of the Nunnes of Syon with the Friores'. A cloak of moral outrage fitted ill that particular king's shoulders, but nothing could save the 'Nunnes' and the 'Friores'. The order was suppressed, the sisters fled to the Low Countries and the abbey became royal property. There, six years later, Henry incarcerated one of his queens, Catherine Howard, before she was beheaded.

In 1547, Henry's own coffined body lay in Syon for a night en route to its burial place at St George's Chapel, Windsor. During the dark hours the casket burst open, and dogs, attracted by the smell, were found licking the corpse. A grim prophecy had been fulfilled: 12 years earlier a Franciscan friar had declared that 'dogs would lick his blood as they had Ahab's.'

Henry had appointed the Duke of Somerset to be protector of his heir. When Prince Edward became king, Somerset secured title to the Syon estate and destroyed all but the underground vaults of the monastery. The house he built in its place provided the Tudor core within which the present Duke of Northumberland lives. In 1552 Somerset was executed for plotting against the crown and John Dudley, Duke of Northumberland, was given the property.

What strange stories attach to great houses! It was at Syon that the gentle, studious Lady Jane Grey was offered the crown by Northumberland, her father-in-law; her father, and other ambitious nobles. She was reluctant, but they persuaded her that, by virtue of her descent from Henry VII (her mother was Henry VII's sister), she and not Henry VIII's daughter, Mary, was the rightful heir. She was taken from Syon by river to the Tower and proclaimed queen – that fateful and pathetic reign which was to last nine days.

The accession of Catholic Mary brought revenge on the Dudleys and the return of the Bridgettines to their abbey. But their stay was brief. When Elizabeth inherited, they were expelled for the second time, drifted through Europe and finally settled in Lisbon. As for Syon, the new queen granted a lease to Henry Percy, ninth Earl of Northumberland. A later Northumberland visited the nuns in Portugal and gave them a silver model of Syon House. When the abbess remarked that she still carried its keys, the duke replied 'Aye, madame, but I have changed the locks since then.' The Bridgettines returned to England in the nineteenth century, and now occupy another Syon Abbey, in Devon.

The last of the male Northumberlands died in 1670, and only his three-year old daughter, Elizabeth survived to inherit. She married three times. Her first husband died at 15, and her second, Thomas Thynne of Longleat, was murdered. The present owners of Syon House descend from the third, Charles, sixth Duke of Somerset, whose grandaughter's husband, Sir Hugh Smithson, was accorded the Northumberland heritage by Act of Parliament in 1750. He and his wife became Earl and Countess and, somewhat later, George III revived the dukedom for him. It is to this duke that we owe Syon House as we see it today.

Rebuilding started in 1762. The architect was Robert Adam. The landscape artist was Lancelot Brown, whose nickname, 'Capability', came from his habitual remark when confronted with an undeveloped piece of land, 'I see great capabilities here.'

To move through Syon House room by room is to move through sheer drenching loveliness. It is not, however, the function of this book to detail its glories. Any printed guide will tell you about the great hall

with its black and white marble floor and its black figure of the Dying
Gaul; the anteroom, the most colourful Adam ever designed, with its
12 ancient green columns dredged up from the bed of the Tiber; the
spacious dining-room with its deep niches containing classical figures
(Adam preferred statues to tapestries where food was served, because
food smells don't cling to stone or marble); the red drawing-room with
its ceiling of octagons and squares and its ten Stuart portraits on the
damasked walls – the first use, as far as is known, of silk as a wall
covering; and the gallery, 136 feet long, whose 11 windows look out
over Capability Brown's sea of greenery.

What is usually omitted from the guides is any mention of a miniscule circular chamber, reached by a secret door at one end of the
gallery. This is known to the family as the birdcage room. You would
not, walking the length of the gallery, guess that it even existed, for
its doorway, like the rest of the room, is painted in arabesques.

This must be the smallest chamber on which Adam ever lavished
so much attention. So incredibly small is it – no more floor space
than that of two or three telephone kiosks – that it was obviously
designed for one person only, and that person presumably the wife
of Adam's employer. Never was there a room so feminine. Its colours
are birds' egg blue, shell-pink and white. Adam's neo-classic plaster
reliefs lead the eye up the curving walls to a domed ceiling, from the
centre of which hangs a golden birdcage containing a golden bird.
The underside of the cage is a clock-face. Everything is impractical
and delicious.

But what was the birdcage room for? For moments during stately
receptions in the gallery when the duchess felt suddenly faint and
wanted to withdraw? For secret romantic trysts? (It would have been
too cramped.) For meditation, reverie? Or could it have been – a less
delightful thought – the duchess's private counting house? The lady
had a way of keeping track of costs. She noted that Pergolesi charged
three guineas each for the 62 pilasters he provided, and that the Dying
Gaul had set the duke back £300. She left to future generations a book,
Prices of Some of the Works Done at Syon. Was it in Adam's secret
room that she composed this chilling compilation?

The nice thing about Syon is that it is still so lived in. The duke's
study is an amiable masculine clutter of books, documents and paintings. The present duchess's sitting-room is intimate and chintzy. It
seems odd to see a television set in the family parlour, but after all,
why not? If TV had existed in the eighteenth century, Adam, with his
devotion to beautifying the functional, would undoubtedly have
designed a suitable cabinet.

If you follow Syon Lane, which leads from the duke's grounds north-west, and then cross the Great West Road, you soon come to a second stretch of open parkland, the grounds of another Adam house, Osterley.

What an extraordinary man was this transplanted Scot, Robert Adam, and how much London and its environs owe to him – not houses and their interior decoration alone, but carpets, bedspreads, door-furniture, tables, chairs, cabinets, candelabra, trophies of arms, friezes in the classic manner, mantels, grates, link-holders. To encompass this enormous range of objects, he relied for the execution of his concepts on one of the most formidable teams ever assembled in the cause of domestic elegance. The foremost of them included Josiah Wedgwood for pottery; Angelica Kauffmann and her husband, Antonio Zucchi, for allegorical painting; Michele Angelo Pergolesi for painted or stucco arabesques; Matthew Boulton for metalwork; Thomas Chippendale for cabinet-making; Thomas Moore for carpets; Joseph Rose for ornamental stucco, plus battalions of craftsmen skilled in all branches of decoration and construction. Like Syon House, Osterley is a monument both to Adam's creative, and to his administrative genius.

No detail was too small for him. There is evidence of this in the state bedchamber at Osterley. Not only did he design the room, the gilt armchairs whose backs are supported by sphinxes, the monarchical four-poster, its coverlet and its valance, but he also designed the carpet. And in that carpet are four spots worked into the pattern. On these spots and nowhere else did he intend that the four legs of the bed should stand – as indeed they do.

In the tapestry room, the carpet accurately echoes the ceiling, for, again, Adam conceived both. In the Etruscan dressing-room, according to the Victoria and Albert Museum, certain of the chairs are 'centrally placed below a painted tripod [part of the wall decoration] so that the painted circular pattern on the splat [of each chair] is repeated in a larger version on the wall immediately above'. Heaven help anyone who ever contemplated re-arranging the furniture!

Osterley, like Syon, presented Adam with the challenge of rebuilding an existing house. He worked on both at the same time, which alone would seem an incredible achievement. But not for this mighty genius. He was, over the same years, also concerned either with rebuilding or building a dozen or more country houses, plus not only a number of town houses in London's most fashionable squares, but a string of 'palazzi' in Portland Place, as well as the Adelphi, the residential development beside the Thames near the Savoy Hotel.

30 *above* Osterley House from the gardens

31 *left* The stairs, Osterley House

Osterley, 'a house becoming a prince', with four square fortress-like turrets, had been built in Elizabeth's day and the queen herself stayed there at least twice. The first time she was the victim of a demonstration by two women who 'maliciously, diabolically and illegally' destroyed the paling that surrounded the grounds, causing her 'great disquiet and disturbance'. On the second visit it was Elizabeth who caused the disquiet by observing that the courtyard 'would appear more handsome if divided with a wall in the middle'. Sir Thomas Gresham, founder of the Royal Exchange, and Osterley's owner, took her comment as a command. He rushed workmen from London while the queen slept, so that all should be to her taste in the morning.

To remark that Osterley, either in its Gresham phase or as later revised by Robert Adam, required a master with a long purse is to assert what would seem obvious. It is less so, however, when one considers how often such estates came into their owners' possession not through careful financial manipulation but through shrewd politicking in one royal court or another. But Gresham was a City man, not a Cecil, a Percy or a Burleigh; and Francis Child, who became Osterley's owner in the eighteenth century, was a goldsmith and, as the founder of Child's Bank near Temple Bar, the father of English banking.

Up to Child's time, rich men had kept their wealth either in their own strongrooms or, less often, with goldsmiths who, having property of their own to guard, presumably knew a bit about the safekeeping of valuables. Child was the first to turn his goldsmithing business into a bank. Through his acumen he rose to a knighthood and became lord mayor of London. He acquired Osterley in 1711; his grandson, another Francis, decided to modernize it. For his architect he hired first Sir William Chambers, and then Adam.

Horace Walpole, ever the amiable inquisitive quidnunc, could hardly wait to see the result, and bustled about Osterley even before the rooms were all finished. He disliked the Etruscan room – 'a potter's field' – and didn't think much of the gardens, but for the most part he was rapturous: 'On Friday we went to see – oh, the palace of palaces! – and yet a palace sans crown, sans coronet, but such expense! such taste! such profusion! . . . The old house . . . is so improved and enriched, that all the Percies and Seymours of Syon must die of envy.'

How Osterley eventually passed out of the Child family and into that of the earls of Jersey, who kept it until 1949 when the ninth earl gave it to the National Trust, is a rollicking romance worthy of Jeffery Farnol or Georgette Heyer. Francis Child died unmarried, and Osterley went to his brother, Robert, whose only heir was a daughter,

Sarah Anne. At 18, she fell in love with John Fane, the tenth Earl of Westmorland, an engaging young man with armorial quarterings far more impressive than his fortune. Knowing that the money-orientated Child would oppose the marriage, he slyly asked Sarah Anne's father while dining with him one night at his house in Berkeley Square, 'Sir, suppose that you were in love with a girl and her father refused his consent to the union. What would you do?'

For a banker, Child was singularly incautious. He replied, 'Do? I should run away with her, to be sure!'

John Fane followed his advice, and early one May morning in 1782, he spirited his love away from Berkeley Square. In a post-chaise, the couple sped north towards Gretna Green. Two of Child's retainers leaped on to a pair of swift hunters in pursuit. As they came abreast of the rocketing carriage, Fane drew a pistol and aimed. But his heart failed him until the indomitable Sarah Anne screamed, 'Shoot, my lord!' Fortunately it was not a man but a horse that was killed, and the post-chaise swept on.

Mr and Mrs Child themselves joined the chase, and somewhere on the Great North Road they began to close the distance between themselves and the runaways. But Fane foiled them too. Coming up with a troop of dragoons whose commanding officer he knew, he asked for help. By the time the Childs reached the spot, the dragoons were spread out across the road, ostensibly engaged in a military exercise. Westmorland and Sarah Anne got clean away and were married 'over the anvil', as the saying goes.

Of the many houses open to visitors in England, Osterley is probably the most satisfying, for it stands exactly as Adam left it, with almost every piece that he designed in place – chairs veneered with rosewood and satinwood, inlaid bombé cabinets, torchères and settees carved and gilded, girandole mirrors, fire baskets, sconces, carpets. The room that fascinates us above all (despite Horace Walpole) is the Etruscan dressing room, whose walls are painted with so-called Etruscan pottery; in actuality, it is Greek, but everyone called it Etruscan then. There was a fad for 'Etruscan' ware at the time, and Josiah Wedgwood was creating pseudo-classic urns and vases for which, he wrote, his London agent was 'mad as a March hare'. Adam considered the apartment a great success, 'a mode of decoration . . . which differs from anything hitherto practised in Europe'. He used it later in five other houses, but only the room at Osterley survives.

Osterley's second delight is the entrance to the courtyard; 12 Ionic columns forming a double portico and supporting the classic pediment of a Grecian temple. This entrance or screen has absolutely nothing in common architecturally with the turreted Elizabethan wings between which it is inserted. The contrast is violent. It is the signature of Robert Adam writ large, an elegant eighteenth-century scrawl across a page of neat Tudor calligraphy.

Polly Adler, late queen of American 'madams', once wrote a book of reminiscence called *A House is Not a Home*. To her, the word 'house' had a peculiarly professional connotation. But when, in a non-Adlerian sense, is a house not a home? The answer may well be when it is called Chiswick House. This exquisite little villa was built not to dwell in, nor necessarily even to eat in, but quite simply as a pleasance, a place in which the best minds of its owner's day might disport themselves in surroundings of the most sophisticated beauty, where his great library could be housed, his pictures hung.

Richard Boyle, third Earl of Burlington, was 35 when, in partnership with William Kent, he completed his temple to good taste at Chiswick, within 200 acres, slightly to the east of Syon. Kent, a superb architect in his own right, attended to most of the inner embellishments; the earl himself designed the building, placing it a few yards from a Jacobean mansion in which he lived.

Burlington was among the first of the generations of English noblemen to make the Grand Tour, and he returned imbued with a passion for the architecture of northern Italy. He transformed his grandfather's mansion in Piccadilly, Burlington House (now, with wings added in the nineteenth century, the home of the Royal Academy), from a red brick Carolean building into an Italianate palace. But in Chiswick House, he turned to a simpler, earlier period.

Both chronologically and spiritually, Chiswick forms a link between Inigo Jones's Banqueting House and Robert Adam's Osterley: all three reflect their architects' fascination with the sixteenth-century villas of Andrea Palladio. Palladio himself was a revivalist, looking back to the buildings of ancient Rome. Inigo Jones, who purchased Palladio's definitive work, *I quattro libri dell' architettura*, in Venice in 1601, brought to England the concept of classicism, the essence of which is its sense of order and symmetry. Chiswick House is an unashamed variant of Palladio's Villa Capra outside Vicenza – domed, with a colonnaded porch flanked by staircases. Adam, though a far more gifted builder than Burlington, still sucked sustenance from Palladio, but in the suaver idiom of his own day.

To Chiswick House came the titans of creativity whom Burlington had in mind when he conceived it – Pope, Handel, John Gay (*The Beggar's Opera* was produced the year before the house was finished),

32 Chiswick House by night

painters, statesmen and the brightest sparks of the court of George II. Burlington willed the house to his heiress's husband, Lord Hartington, who became the fourth Duke of Devonshire. His successor hired James Wyatt to enlarge it – wings were added north and south – and under the Devonshire sway, which lasted until the end of the nineteenth century, the pleasance functioned less as a centre of artistic than of political talent. Charles James Fox was a frequent visitor and died there in 1806. Twenty-one years later, George Canning also breathed his last in Chiswick House.

In the nineteenth century it became a good pull-up for monarchs. Lord Melbourne met the czar there, and on 19 June 1844, he wrote to Queen Victoria that it was 'extremely fortunate that a sovereign of such weight and influence in Europe . . . should also be a man upon whose honour and veracity strong reliance may be safely and securely placed.'

Edward VII, when he was Prince of Wales, borrowed Chiswick House from the heir to the dukedom, Lord Hartington, whom Bertie nicknamed 'Harty-Tarty'. During the prince's time the villa almost

33 *above* Kenwood House

34 *right* The Library, Kenwood

caused an international imbroglio. When Napoleon III was overthrown after France's defeat by Prussia, the Empress Eugénie and her son sought sanctuary in England. The Prince of Wales offered her Chiswick House, but Gladstone's government, about to recognize the new French republic, were furious, and Victoria rebuked her son for rocking the diplomatic boat. It was pretty Eugénie herself who saved Bertie from further embarrassment by tactfully refusing his offer.

By 1892 the days of distinction were over. The duke removed his paintings to Chatsworth, and debonair little Chiswick House became a lunatic asylum. Eventually Lord Burlington's charming whim was acquired by the Middlesex County Council and was opened to the public.

A few years ago it was completely restored and redecorated in the colours Kent had used, although flock wallpaper has replaced the original fabric in the red, blue and green velvet rooms. Some of the Chatsworth pictures have been re-hung in their original places in the domed saloon. But Chiswick House, alas, is bare of furniture and a trifle sad. Sunlight streams through the high arched windows, bringing a semblance of life to the gilt adornments of mantels and ceilings. Yet the exquisite rooms echo emptily. The house cries out, almost piteously, for a tenant of taste and nobility. The authorities have done their best, but no sleeping beauty was ever awakened by a kiss from an urban district council.

Nowhere in London is the purity of classicism better exemplified than at Kenwood, at the northern end of Hampstead Heath, the hilltop home of William Murray, later lord chief justice and first Earl of Mansfield. A Scot himself, he hired his fellow Scot, the omnipresent Robert Adam, to reconstruct the seventeenth-century house he had bought. Adam's south front, three storeys high, with a one-storey wing to either side, is the quintessence of ordered symmetry. And the house's positioning is as happy as its proportions. Standing on the grassy terrace that slopes gently from the south façade, you can, on a clear day, see what is probably the finest view of London to be had from any vantage point.

On the broad flatness of Oxford Street or Kensington High Street, you are apt to forget that London lies in a river valley. From Regent's Park northwards, it is all uphill to Hampstead, Parliament Hill Fields and at last to the Heath and Kenwood House, which stands in cool serenity against a backdrop of dark trees. Below the terrace the ground swoops sharply down to ornamental lakes with ducks and swans and kingfishers like those in the reeds along the young Thames where it meanders through Oxfordshire. By night, owls hoot and you can hear the nightingales' threnody, just as Keats heard it on the southern side of the Heath; among the shadows, foxes venture forth, and badgers. No naturalist has yet reported stumbling across a sleeping Titania or spying Bottom in his ass's head. But Kenwood at moonrise may still have secrets to guard.

The first Kenwood – or Cane Wood, as it was called – was built in James I's day by the royal printer, John Bill. This house was pulled down in the early 1700s and replaced by another which passed through six or seven hands until Lord Mansfield bought it as his country retreat. He lived for the most part in his town house in Bloomsbury Square, within handy distance of Lincoln's Inn and the Court of King's Bench.

He was reputed a hard, though never a hanging judge. The decision which won him the most fame – it certainly stirred up the hottest controversy – involved a black slave named James Somerset who had been brought to England, run away and been recaptured by his owner, Charles Stewart, of Virginia. This was a common enough occurrence and the affair might have gone unnoticed had it not been for the first of England's abolitionists, Granville Sharp. In his view, slavery on English soil (as distinct from the soil of England's colonies) was illegal, since no law specifically authorized the institution. He had, for seven years, argued this contention unsuccessfully through a string of law cases.

Lord Mansfield, though sympathetic with those who believed in the sanctity of property, and genuinely worried about the future of thousands of blacks who, if freed, might be without means of subsistence, nevertheless recognized the legality of Sharp's claim. But he needed a clean-cut case in which one man in England asserted ownership of another. The Somerset contretemps proved the ideal vehicle. Lord Mansfield summarized his findings on 22 June 1772, after a tense battle in the Court of King's Bench. With it, slavery received its first significant setback:

. . . So high an act of dominion [of one man over another] must be recognized by the law of the country where it is used . . . The state of slavery is of such a nature, that it is incapable of being introduced on any reasons, moral or political, but only by positive law . . . It is so odious, that nothing can be suffered to support it, but positive law. Whatever inconveniences, therefore, may follow from the decision, I cannot say this case is allowed or approved by the law of England; and therefore the black must be discharged.'

35 Apsley House: No. 1, London

Such was the man, calm, prudent, courageous, for whom Robert Adam created calm, prudent, remote Kenwood House. From here Mansfield could survey the turbulence of London far below as from his bench he could survey the turbulence of human affairs. He regarded the house as a part-time retreat from the City while he served as a judge, and as an eventual retirement home for himself and his wife; they were childless. But unruly mankind speeded up his plans.

In 1780, anti-papist demonstrations – the Gordon Riots – erupted and, because Mansfield had several times ruled in favour of persecuted Catholics, the rioters saw in him their sworn enemy. They sacked his Bloomsbury home and he and Lady Mansfield, fleeing just ahead of the flames, set off for Kenwood. The mob galloped after them, intent on wrecking the hilltop house as well. But when they reached the Spaniard's Inn, that cheerful old pub at the edge of Hampstead Heath on the road to Kenwood, the landlord plied them with beer and spirits until they were too drunk to go on. The inn is still there and, thanks to its wily eighteenth-century host, so is Kenwood.

There is poetic justice in the fact that since Lord Mansfield's library in Bloomsbury was completely destroyed, the library at Kenwood should be the finest room in the house. The word 'poetic' in this instance is accurate, for many experts consider this the finest room that Adam ever built, the most rhythmically balanced. Long and narrow with a flat arched ceiling ('much more perfect', wrote Adam, 'than that which is commonly called the cove ceiling'), it forms one of the two low wings. The other is an orangery.

The furniture that Adam designed, not only for this chamber but for the rest of the house, was scattered in 1922, some sold at auction and the rest transported to the Mansfield family seat, Scone Palace, in Scotland. Kenwood had been handed down through a nephew, Viscount Stormont, second Earl of Mansfield, who was 66 when he inherited it. Although he and the generations immediately following cherished the house and added to its fabric and its furnishings, by the twentieth century the eyes of the Mansfields were turning more and more to Scotland.

It was the sixth earl who decided to give Kenwood up altogether and to stay permanently at Scone. Either the upkeep of the beautiful house and its grounds was too burdensome, or he cared little for them. Fortunately others did. A Kenwood Preservation Council was formed, which bought part of the grounds in 1922, and three years later, Edward Cecil Guinness, first Earl of Iveagh, bought the house and the 74 acres immediately surrounding it. He refurnished it (some period pieces have been purchased, some are on loan from titled families) and installed a collection of paintings which are typical of what an eighteenth-century gentleman would have owned. Then he bequeathed the entire estate to the public.

There could be no sharper contrast than that between the somnolence of Kenwood and the snarl and grumble of traffic at Hyde Park Corner. Yet it is in the midst of this vehicular whirligig that the last of inner London's great houses still in family occupation stands. Apsley House, the home of the first Duke of Wellington, and now of his descendants, predates the Iron Duke himself. When it was built, it was the most westerly of Mayfair's many mansions. But now it stands isolated. Some years ago city planners knocked down several neighbouring houses and bulldozed a road through from Piccadilly to Park Lane, leaving the dignified place, with its butterscotch-coloured walls of Bath stone, stranded like the hulk of a ship, high and dry on a reef.

A snippet of folklore attaches to the origin of the property. One day in the late 1740s, King George II was riding along what was then the Bath Road, en route to Knightsbridge village when he noticed a man in the tattered remnants of a soldier's coat standing at the wayside. George, the last English king to lead his troops into battle – at Dettingen, in the War of the Austrian Succession – had considerable affection for the army. He stopped and struck up a conversation with the ragged stranger.

His name was Allen and, by a happy coincidence, he had actually fought at Dettingen. He now scratched a living selling apples, and his home was a tumbledown shack nearby. The king asked how he could help, and Allen replied that he was under constant threat of eviction by his landlord, a rascally innkeeper. Could the threat be removed? George made a note of the case and arranged for the freehold to be transferred to the old soldier and his heirs forever.

Where Allen's hut stood, Apsley House stands today. There is probably no more valuable site in all London. Allen's son grew up to become an attorney, prospered and eventually sold a lease of the land to the lord chancellor, Lord Apsley. He commissioned (it seems inevitable) Robert Adam to build him a stately home of red brick. In 1810, Marquess Wellesley, the Duke of Wellington's younger brother, purchased the lease, and in 1816, a year after Waterloo, the duke himself moved in, buying the lease from his brother. In 1820, the nation acquired the freehold and gave it, as a mark of gratitude, to the victor of Waterloo. So enormous was the esteem in which he was held that Apsley House soon became known as 'Number One, London'. During his period the house was enlarged and the stone facing added.

The entire neighbourhood is filled with memories of Wellington. The Achilles statue not far away in Hyde Park was erected in his honour 'by the women of England' and is made of metal recovered from enemy cannon his armies had captured at the battles of Salamanca, Vittoria, Toulouse and Waterloo. In Old Barrack Yard, a mews behind the Berkeley Hotel, is a little pub, the Grenadier (the only pub in London with a pewter-topped bar), which was once Wellington's officers' mess. The duke kept his horses in the same mews, and his mounting-block is still there.

Apsley House itself is both shrine and museum. The duke's original dispatch detailing the Waterloo victory, and edited in his own hand, is there. So is his iron bed, calculated to mortify all but the most stubborn flesh. In the stair-well stands a gigantic nude of Napoleon by Canova; since Wellington left the emperor militarily stripped, the statue makes a wry and apposite point. The duke's picture collection, like virtually everything else in the house, recalls the rumble of war. Several of the paintings had been seized by Joseph Bonaparte from the royal Spanish collection and then, after the trumph at Vittoria, seized by Wellington in his turn from Joseph's travelling carriage.

Later he offered to return them to the king of Spain, but the king refused, saying that the duke had come into their possession 'by means as just as they were honourable'.

VII
PEOPLE AND PLACES

WHEREVER you wander in London, memories of the famous jog your elbow. Some 350 of the houses where they lived are marked with round blue plaques, brief digests of monumental lives. In many flats over many years we have had distinguished neighbours of the past. In the Bayswater Road we were almost next door to one of Sir James Barrie's three London homes, and only steps away from the Peter Pan statue in Kensington Gardens which was erected secretly in the quiet darkness of one night to surprise the children next morning. In Cadogan Place we were a few doors from the house where William Wilberforce died, not far from Noël Coward's home in Gerald Road and within easy walk of Ebury Street, where Mozart, aged eight, wrote his first symphony and George Moore wrote *Conversations in Ebury Street*. In Palace Gate we were 50 yards and 75 years distant from the marbled mansion Millais had built for himself, with a 40-foot studio, large enough not only for his own current works but to hang a gigantic canvas by Van Dyck.

Our flat in the Adelphi was John Galsworthy's in his pre-Forsyte days. It had no less than five mantels by Robert Adam and a blue-and-white ceiling in the Wedgwood manner, designed by Flaxman. Our friends used to lie on the floor to enjoy it. Galsworthy loved that mid-London retreat. When he moved north to the heights of Hampstead in September 1918, he wrote in his diary, 'Removed from Adelphi Terrace to Grove Lodge. So ended our tenancy of the little Adelphi flat, which will be chiefly remembered for its closeness to Barrie, its dinners at Romano's, the war and air raids. We leave it just as peace is coming.'

The Adelphi, from the Greek *adelphoi* – brothers – was named for

36 26 Dean Street, Karl Marx's home 1851–56

the brothers Adam, of whom there were four, all in varying degrees engaged in the family architectural firm. Besides Robert, the acknowledged genius, only James participated on the creative side, and the two were responsible for the ambitious scheme 'to raise palaces upon an offensive heap of mud'. They laid out an enclave of comely streets and named them for the family: John, Robert, James, William and Adam Streets, with a fine row of houses raised on arches overhanging the Thames embankment which they called Adelphi Terrace.

Sadly, almost all of the terrace and the heart of the enclave were pulled down in 1936 and replaced by an ugly office building. But Robert Street, John Adam Street and Adam Street remain, with enough of the classical frontages to tell us what it must have been like in happier days.

The houses facing the river were fashionably tenanted from the start. David Garrick moved in, and so did Dr Johnson's friends, Topham and Lady Diana Beauclerk, he a descendant of Charles II and Nell Gwyn and a man-about-town and book collector, and she, daughter of the second Duke of Marlborough, and an artist. Robert Adam himself lived next door to the Beauclerks, until he moved around the corner into the street he had named for himself. About a century later Richard D'Oyly Carte took over Robert Adam's first house. At roughly the same time a young man named Thomas Hardy was studying with an architect who had offices in the terrace and doodling caricatures in pencil on the white marble mantels. He had by then already published *Under the Greenwood Tree*, but he was a Wessex man at heart and his major novels were written after he went back to his beloved West Country.

George Bernard Shaw lived at the corner of the terrace and Robert Street for 30 years, and some of his best plays – *Candida, Caesar and Cleopatra, Major Barbara, Pygmalion* and *Saint Joan* among others – date from those days. He delighted in the fact that the Adelphi was so secret (you can walk along the Strand without realizing that it's hidden behind it) and said, 'I live in the heart of London, miles from anywhere.'

James Barrie came to his third-floor flat at Number 3, Robert Street, opposite Shaw's, in 1911, and installed in the exquisite drawing-room a 'crofter's fireplace' made of rough stone. The two playwrights used to toss biscuits or cherry stones across the street at each other's windows when one had a guest he thought the other would like to see. Barrie's flat has become business offices, but the fireplace is still there.

About a century before the Adelphi rose, Samuel Pepys had chambers one street away in York Buildings (now Buckingham Street), first at Number 12, with his clerk, William Hewer, and then at Number

14, where he stayed until 1699. During this period he laboured both in parliament and in the Navy Office. And here he wrote his second diary, so lacking in vivacity compared with his first. His beloved wife had died and, although he had taken a young mistress, Mary Skinner, his writing was dispirited. Perhaps he was reflecting not only the fact that he himself was aging, but that the buoyant years of the Restoration had long since been replaced by the stodgy reign of William and Mary.

Dickens knew the Adelphi well; he worked nearby as a child in a blacking warehouse close to the present Charing Cross Station. His memories are distilled in *David Copperfield*: 'I was fond of wandering about the Adelphi because it was a mysterious place with those dark arches. I see myself emerging one evening . . . on a little public-house close to the river, with an open space before it, where some coal-heavers were dancing. . . .' Later, David Copperfield's aunt, Betsey Trotwood, set him up in his first bachelor flat in the house at the south-west corner of Buckingham Street.

Kipling came to the region when he was 24 and climbed seven flights to his top-floor rooms in Embankment Chambers, 43 Villiers Street. The building is now called Kipling House. From his windows he could see the Charing Cross railway bridge over the Thames, and Gatti's Music Hall on the west side of Villiers Street. He lived on sausages and mashed potatoes bought for tuppence from Harris, the Sausage King, who ran a tatty eating-place downstairs. Kipling wrote *The Light That Failed* in Villiers Street, and his hero, Dick Heldar (he also went through a sausage-and-mash period), occupied Kipling's own rooms:

'The chambers stood much higher than the other houses commanding a hundred chimneys – crooked cowls that looked like sitting cats as they swung around. . . . Northward the lights of Piccadilly Circus and Leicester Square threw a copper-coloured glare above the black roofs, and southward lay all the orderly lights of the Thames. A train rolled out across one of the railway bridges, and its thunder drowned for a moment the sullen roar of the streets. The Nilghai looked at his watch and said shortly: "That's the Paris night-mail. You can book from here to St Petersburg if you choose."'

Parallel to Villiers Street but on the western side of Charing Cross Station is Craven Street, in which what is now a shabby little eighteenth-century house, Number 36, was twice the home of Benjamin Franklin. He came there first in 1757, representing the General Assembly of Pennsylvania, and complained in a letter to his wife, 'The whole town is one great smoky house, and every street a chimney, the air full of

37 *left* 41 Beak Street, where Canaletto lived

38 *below* Dining room of Dr Johnson's house, Gough Square

floating sea coal soot. . . .' His second stay began a decade later and
lasted half a dozen years, during which he tried not only to fend off
the American Revolution with vain efforts to convince parliament to
ease the taxes that were so exacerbating the colonists, but also conduct-
ing studies into sun spots, the aurora borealis and the feasibility of
equipping St Paul's Cathedral with lightning rods.

The slope upwards from the river continues beyond the Strand to
Covent Garden, Drury Lane and Bow Street. Here those renowned
early police, the Bow Street Runners, came into being: the Bow Street
Magistrates' Court is still a temporary way-station for evil-doers who
are tried at last in the Old Bailey. Charles Lamb lived at 20 Russell
Street, which crosses Bow Street, in the period of the 'Robin Red-
breasts', as the Runners were called because of their scarlet waistcoats,
and he noted that his sister Mary 'had not been here four and twenty
hours before she saw a thief. She sits at the window working, and,
casually throwing out her eyes, she sees a concourse of people coming
this way with a constable to conduct the solemnity. These little
incidents agreeably diversify a female life.'
    One block from Covent Garden, at 60–61 St Martin's Lane,
Thomas Chippendale produced his furniture. Just beyond, in an
octagonal studio in Leicester Square, Joshua Reynolds painted some
of his most important canvasses. And to the north of Leicester Square
is Lisle Street, where Soho begins.
    Like Bloomsbury, Mayfair and several other distinctive areas, Soho
is delimited not by geographical lines, but rather by temperament.
The purists say that it is contained within the four circuses, Piccadilly,
Oxford, Cambridge and St Giles. But since it is a realm of the spirit,
no one is really certain where it stops and starts. Its denizens have a
rag-tag dignity. A vagrant lady known locally as 'the Countess' found
a sequinned evening dress in a dust-bin one twilight, walked into a
churchyard and took off her own shabby dress. She was slipping into
the gown when a bobby arrived. 'What do you think you're doing?'
he asked brusquely. She replied, 'What every other lady in London
is doing at this hour. Changing for dinner!'
    'Soho', wrote Galsworthy in *The Forsyte Saga*, is 'untidy, full of
Greeks, Ishmaelites, Italians, tomatoes, restaurants, organs [and]
coloured stuffs [and] dwells remote from the British body politic.'
Soho was and is a mile-square island of foreignness. Immigrant
restaurateurs, shopkeepers and craftsmen have huddled together in this
quarter for generations, swept in by successive waves of war and terror
on the Continent.

Greek refugees fled there and are remembered in Greek Street. French Huguenots sought shelter there during the sixteenth and seventeenth centuries. Theodore, the last king of Corsica, hastened from his perfumed island to 4 Great Chapel Street and there, burdened with debts for which he pledged his lost kingdom, he died. A Soho oil merchant paid for his funeral. He lies buried in the churchyard of ruined St Anne's in Wardour Street.

Karl Marx arrived in Soho after being hounded out of Germany and France, and lived in poverty with his family at 26 Dean Street. The building now houses Leoni's Quo Vadis, an Italian restaurant, whose proprietor once came upon, in Marx's old rooms, a small cache of books heavily annotated in German, volumes the revolutionary no doubt used in preparing *Das Kapital*, which he researched in the Reading Room of the British Museum. Marx's grave is in Highgate Cemetery, a shrine for communists from all over the world.

There is scarcely a nationality not represented within Soho, mostly in trades involving eating and drinking. A recent influx from Hong Kong has made of several of its crowded noisy streets a miniature Chinatown, with mahogany-skinned ducks festooning restaurant windows, and supermarkets that specialize in bean curds, aged eggs, water chestnuts and the like. Of late, however, the attractions of Soho in general have gradually shifted from the gastronomic to the pornographic – one-girl brothels, strip clubs, massage parlours.

Cosmopolitan, sleazy and strangely lovable – behind the tangle of it all are memories which bequeathed to Soho not only its down-at-heel magic, but also its air of a tatterdemalion Bohemia.

In the 1870s, both Verlaine and Rimbaud read their poems to their friends in a bar at 5 Old Compton Street. Verlaine, like most of his countrymen, was both frightened and baffled by London: 'Groups of buildings in squares, courts and shut-in terraces from which the cabmen are driven. Parks that show nature improved with consummate art. The fashionable quarters full of things past understanding; an arm of sea, empty of ships, tumbling its mane of slatey spume between embankments loaded with huge candelabra.'

Although neither he nor Rimbaud knew the city, the instinct that led them to Old Compton Street was sound, for not far away, at 28 Broadwick Street, a far greater poet, William Blake, had been born and spent the first 25 years of his life. As a young man, he sold his engravings at Number 27. A year before Blake's birth a Venetian artist who called himself Canaletto arrived in Soho and moved into a cramped brick house, 41 Beak Street. Soon he offered to the public 'A View of St James's Park which he hopes may in some Measure deserve their Appreciation'. He stayed in England for seven years, painting many studies of London in his meticulously detailed yet fresh and airy style – aspects of the Thames, St Paul's, the pleasure gardens at Ranelagh.

In the eighteenth century Soho was a mixture of hovels and mansions – room for the affluent as well as the hunted and hungry. During the 1760s a comely Italian, Theresa Cornelys, descended on Soho Square in a flurry of perfume and flexible morality to launch a lurid career. Madame Cornelys, known successively as Madame Pompeati, Madame Trenti and the Sultana of Soho, had trod the stages and rumpled the beds (Casanova fathered her daughter) of various European capitals before winding up in Carlisle House, an aristocratic old building, where she staged a series of pay-as-you-enter routs. To these costume balls came England's aristocracy, foreign ambassadors, celebrities like Garrick, Sheridan, Goldsmith and Reynolds. One man turned up as Death, dressed in a winding sheet, and the Duchess of Kingston came as Iphigenia, 'in a state almost ready for the sacrifice', as Walpole commented.

The homes of European political figures, most but not all refugees, are scattered widely through London. Lenin lived at 16 Finsbury Circus, where he published his revolutionary magazine, *Iskra*, whose slogan was 'From Spark to Flame'. There he first joined forces with Trotsky. Giuseppe Mazzini, the Italian patriot, escaped to England in 1837 and lived first in Goodge Street and later at 183 Gower Street. He founded a school in Hatton Garden for indigent Italian organ-grinders. 'These poor devils', he wrote, 'go about with their organs all day and then, if they have a penny to spare, wander into a public house and drink till they fall asleep.'

World War II brought a fresh crop of wanderers: Charles de Gaulle, King George of the Hellenes, Queen Wilhelmina of the Netherlands, Jan Masaryk of Czechoslovakia. The monarchs stayed mostly in Mayfair, their first haven often Claridge's Hotel.

Mayfair, one of the world's most prestigious and most copied place names, derives from one of London's rowdiest old events, an annual cattle market, the May Fair, which drew buskers, jugglers, gamblers and guzzlers. It began in the reign of James II, but was closed down by Queen Anne as 'a publick nuisance [where] many loose, idle and disorderly persons do . . . allure young persons and servants to game and commit lewd and disorderly practices'. The fair had a brief resurgence under the early Hanovers, but by then the neighbourhood had already become too stylish for livestock sales, conners and swanners.

The new tone had been set in Charles II's time, when his lord chancellor, Edward Hyde, Earl of Clarendon, built a conspicuous mansion with a sweeping view down toward St James's Palace on the site where now Old Bond Street runs into Piccadilly. Clarendon fled into exile under threat of impeachment by parliament for alleged malfeasance; a short while later his house was torn down and Bond Street, Dover Street, Albemarle Street and Stafford Street laid out. Property development spread swiftly over the fields to the north, and by 1729, a rhymester, resenting the loss of the Maypole and the fields of 'peases, cabbages and turnips', lamented,

> *Such piles of building now rise up and down,*
> *London itself seems growing out of town.*

By the 1800s, Mayfair had become what it remained almost until our own time, the most snobbish quarter in London. Within it, wrote Sydney Smith, was 'more intelligence, human ability, to say nothing of wealth and beauty than the world ever collected in so small a space before.'

Handel wrote *The Messiah* at 25 Brook Street. Number 46 Berkeley Square became the home of Lord Clive of India, and Number 11, directly across the square, was Horace Walpole's town house. On the south-west corner of the square, Robert Adam built Lansdowne House for the Earl of Bute, George III's first prime minister. The house underwent numerous changes of ownership: Gordon Selfridge, the American department-store tycoon, rented it during the 1920s at £5,000 a year, and threw parties with jazz bands at which the flappers of the first mini-skirt era Charlestoned energetically. Subsequently it endured architectural butchery but, unlike most of Mayfair's other mansions, it at least survived. It is now the Lansdowne Club and several of Adam's rooms are still there, the proportions and plaster-work as he conceived them, but fearsomely repainted.

Nelson lived in Bond Street, at Number 147, during the bitterest period of his life, a grim grey winter. He had lost his right eye at Calvi. His right arm, which had been shattered by grapeshot during a battle in the Canaries and clumsily amputated by a ship's surgeon, caused him great pain. He felt, as he confided to Admiral Lord St Vincent, 'dead to the world' and 'useless to my country'. But gradually he regained his strength, and when he raised his anchor again, a blazing spirit in a fragile veil of flesh, the Nile and Trafalgar still lay before him – two last victories and the cold salt lash of seaborne immortality.

Perhaps because it has always been expensive, Mayfair has never sheltered large colonies of writers, as have Bloomsbury, the Adelphi,

39 *right* Disraeli lived at No. 19 Curzon
Street

40 *below* Keats's house, Hampstead

41 *above* The London home of Mark Twain, No. 23 Tedworth Square

42 *left* Carlyle's house, 24 Cheyne Row

Chelsea and Kensington. In his old age, Dr Johnson stayed in Grosvenor Square with his friends, the Thrales; but Fleet Street was his natural milieu, and there he laboured on his dictionary for more than a decade with a team of amanuenses in the attic of his house (now a museum) in Gough Square, off Wine Office Court. Boswell was attracted by Mayfair's butterfly glamour and drifted briefly from one lodging to the next – in Half Moon Street, in Bond Street, in Piccadilly.

Benjamin Disraeli was a Mayfair man to his well-polished fingernails. He married at St George's, Hanover Square, moved into his wife's house at Grosvenor Gate, Park Lane, and, after her death, bought the lease of 19 Curzon Street with £10,000 he earned from his last novel, *Endymion*. Both houses still stand, unspoiled. Disraeli died in Curzon Street in the spring of 1881, cheered towards the end by primroses that his greatest admirer, Queen Victoria, sent him from Windsor.

Charles Dickens, who used to walk endless miles exploring London, and said, 'I suppose myself to know this large city as well as anyone in it', had little rapport with Mayfair. His chief association there was with Clarendon's Hotel (long vanished), where he would go to meet the wealthy Baroness Burdett-Coutts whom he advised on her charity donations. He himself had 32 different London addresses, and considered the city a 'magic lantern' for his writing. He was 11 when his parents came from Chatham to 16 Bayham Street, Camden Town, 'about the poorest part of London then', he wrote years later, 'and the house was a mean small tenement with a wretched little back garden abutting on a squalid court.'

Shortly afterwards he lived alone in Lant Street, Southwark, while his father, the prototype of Micawber, was in a debtors' prison nearby. In *David Copperfield*, he recalled the place: 'There is a repose about Lant Street, in the Borough, which sheds a gentle melancholy upon the soul. . . . If a man wished to abstract himself from the world . . . to place himself beyond the possibility of any inducement to look out of the window, we should recommend him by all means to go to Lant Street.'

By the time he took his bride to Furnival's Inn, Holborn (since torn down to make way for the Prudential Assurance), he was already famous as 'Boz'. He began *The Pickwick Papers* there and finished them at 21 Doughty Street, Bloomsbury, where he also wrote *Oliver Twist* and started *Nicholas Nickleby*. The house is preserved as a museum, and you can see the tall clerk's desk where he wrote standing up, often while chatting with guests in the room. In a study opening on to a garden at 1 Devonshire Place (now a business block), he produced *Barnaby Rudge, The Old Curiosity Shop, Martin Chuzzlewit, A Christmas Carol, Dombey and Son* and most of *David Copperfield*. Number 1, Tavistock Square, Bloomsbury, was the birthplace of *Little Dorrit* and *Bleak House*.

Some of his fictional London locations are precise. City business-men today lunch on steaks and chops in the old George and Vulture, in a dog-leg alley, George Court, where Mr Pickwick and Sam Weller stayed. Pip's rooms were on the top floor of 'the last house down by the river' in the Temple, and Tiny Tim's home was probably modelled on Bayham Street. But other placings are vague, and have been the subject of literary detective work.

In tracking some of them down, we discovered that the much-touted Old Curiosity Shop near Lincoln's Inn Fields, though un-doubtedly venerable, was definitely not the original; that was in Orange Street, near Leicester Square. As for Fagin's den, he put it in Saffron Hill: 'A dirtier or more wretched place [Oliver Twist] had never seen. The street was very narrow and muddy, and the air was impregnated with many filthy odours. . . . Covered ways and yards, which here and there diverged from the main street, disclosed little knots of houses, where drunken men and women were positively wallowing in filth.' But he did not pinpoint the building.

To do so, we consulted an extraordinary map drawn in 1792 by Richard Horwood, in which every house is individually numbered. At the foot of Saffron Hill a street called Chick Lane (or sometimes West Street) ran into what is now Holborn Circus and bridged the Fleet Ditch, on whose west bank is a house numbered 'three'. It had first been a tavern and then a hideout for criminals. A chronicler of local history wrote, 'Its dark closets, trap-doors, sliding panels and secret recesses rendered it one of the most secure places for robbery and murder.' There is little doubt that this was Dickens's model.

The wicked house has vanished and Saffron Hill today is less squalid than dull. By night, however, with the street lamps reflecting streaks of rain from rough old walls, it still seems sinister. Much of Hatton Garden, to which poor Oliver was dragged to be tried before the dreadful magistrate, Mr Fang, remains as Dickens knew it, save that it has since become the world's centre of diamond-trading.

Fictional characters are often as real as their creators. You can trace the Forsytes, from Old Jolyon's mansion in Stanhope Gate, Park Lane, to Timothy's in the Bayswater Road and Soames's sorrowful ménage with Irene in Montpelier Square, Sherlock Holmes undoubtedly played his fiddle and solved his crimes at 221b Baker Street, even though no such street number ever existed. And it is far easier to envisage Robinson Crusoe and his man Friday on their island than it is Daniel Defoe writing about them in his gloomy red brick house at 95 Stoke Newington Church Street.

Although most of London's suburbs have been scorned by the talented and the renowned (George Eliot, who worked on *The Mill on the Floss* at 31 Wimbledon Park Road, is one of the outstanding exceptions), the winding pretty streets of Hampstead have always enticed them. There Keats wrote most of his best-known poems, including *Ode to a Nightingale*, in what is now a museum called Keats House, in Keats Grove. Constable painted 'one of my best pictures' at 6 (now 40) Well Walk, whose drawing-room commanded 'a view unsurpassed in Europe, from Westminster Abbey to Greenwich.' George Romney had a studio on Holly Bush Hill, and Dr Johnson wrote *The Vanity of Human Wishes* in a street named Frognal. Kate Greenaway, the writer and illustrator of children's books, spent the last 16 years of her life at Number 39 in the same street. H. G. Wells, after many years in Hampstead's trim, prim Church Row, moved southward to Regent's Park and settled at 13 Hanover Terrace, one of Nash's statuesque parkside houses, the colour of rich clotted cream. Here he died.

The story of London, like that of Paris, is of a gradual drift westward of the *beau monde* – from Mayfair through Belgravia to the old villages of Chelsea, Kensington, Fulham and Chiswick. Chelsea and Kensington are now, for administrative purposes, welded into a single borough; further to compound the topographical confusion, a finger of Westminster juts from the east into Kensington. But it *looks* like Kensington, it feels like Kensington and (*pace* all borough pedants), by God it is Kensington! The boundary line is marked by a stone in the back garden of the Israeli embassy, at 2 Palace Green.

This house was built for William Makepeace Thackeray, and it was his last home. Earlier he had lived at 36 Onslow Square and at 16 Young Street, which runs between Kensington High Street and Kensington Square. He chose the Young Street house because its bulging bay windows 'had the air of a feudal castle'. It was there that he wrote his masterpiece, and once, walking along the street with a friend, he exclaimed, 'Down on your knees, you rogue, for here *Vanity Fair* was penned.' He added, 'I will go down with you, for I have a high opinion of that little production myself.'

Kensington, quietly comfortable and basking smugly in the cachet of having been designated 'the Royal Borough' by grant of Edward VII, has long been one of London's chief nuclei for top people – literary,

artistic, political. To name a few: G. K. Chesterton was born at 11
Warwick Gardens, where he first flexed his literary muscles:

> *. . . A child I dreamed, and dream it still,*
> *Under the great grey water-tower*
> *That strikes the stars on Campden Hill.*

Henry James wrote *The Turn of the Screw* and *The Spoils of Poynton*
at 34 De Vere Gardens; Talleyrand stayed briefly at 11 Kensington
Square, and was a devotee of the influential salons at Holland House;
Winston Churchill ended his days in Hyde Park Gate.

But for name-dropping purposes, Chelsea is even better. We are
haunted by a meeting which never occurred and never could have,
between Oscar Wilde, who lived at 16 Tite Street (now 34) and Mark
Twain, who stayed around the corner at 23 Tedworth Square. They
could never have crossed paths because by 1896, when Twain came
to Chelsea, Wilde was already in Reading Goal. Yet the imagined
meeting persists in the mind, between two of the most colossal talents
of their time – indeed, of any time – both at the dismal nadir of their
fortunes.

It would be an evening of dense fog, sweeping up from the river.
Curtains would be drawn against the unfriendly night. Then along
Tite Street towards the square, swinging his gold-headed malacca
cane, would come Oscar Wilde, stout, almost gross, extravagantly
dressed, outwardly jaunty. But the face would be twisted with grief.
He would turn the corner just as Mark Twain came down his front
steps. In the fog the pair would carom into each other. The creator
of *Huckleberry Finn* would raise his hat to the creator of *Dorian Gray*.
Then each would pursue his lonely way into the mist.

The house in Tite Street, with its ultra-fashionable William Morris
wallpaper, Japanese vases, Whistler etchings and beaded curtains,
was Wilde's pride, but with his downfall, all his possessions were
auctioned to satisfy his debts. His son, Vyvyan Holland, recalled those
gruelling days: 'Even before [the sale] took place, the house was full
of riff-raff souvenir-hunting and stealing. . . . Books of inestimable
value for their association interest were sold in bundles of twenty or
thirty for two or three pounds. . . . Among them were first editions of
all my father's books with inscriptions to my mother, to my brother
and to myself. . . . For months afterwards, my brother and I kept
asking for our soldiers, our trains and other toys, and we could not
understand why it upset our mother. . . . It was only when I saw the
catalogue, many years later, that I realized. . . . The sale consisted of

of 246 lots; number 237 was "A large quantity of toys"; they realized thirty shillings.'

Mark Twain's temporary refuge also still stands – red brick, glum, subtly sorrowful. His golden days were over when he moved there. He had lost his showpiece home in Hartford, Connecticut and, bankrupt, had set out for Europe to retrieve his fortunes and pay off his creditors. He was away from the United States for nine years, and in Tedworth Square he toiled over the only bad book he ever wrote, *Following the Equator*. His nights were horrible, riven by dreams of a curiosly obscene quality: '. . . a negro wench . . . shiny black eyes . . . thick lips . . . she had but one garment on – a coarse tow-linen shirt. . . . She made a disgusting proposition to me.'

He was rumoured to be ill, dying. The London correspondent of the *New York Journal* went to see him; he was to cable 500 words if the author were ill, 1,000 if he were dead. Twain received him with a grim smile and the reply (often misquoted): 'The report of my death is an exaggeration.' He left Tedworth Square the following summer.

If Chelsea has a patron saint, other than St Thomas More who lived near the river in Henry VIII's time, it is surely Thomas Carlyle, essayist, historian, conversationalist, 'the Sage of Chelsea'. His home, 24 Cheyne Row, a quiet side-street running off the embankment, is probably London's most complete literary museum: even one of the author's broad-brimmed black hats hangs on a peg near the door to the garden. The building dates from Queen Anne's time, and the new occupant wrote on 21 May 1834, 'I feel a great liking for this excellent old house. . . . We . . . are a "genteel neighbourhood", two old ladies on the one side, unknown character on the other. . . . The house itself is eminent, antique; wainscotted to the very ceiling . . . broadish stair with massive balustrade . . . floors firm as a rock . . . thrice the strength of a modern floor.'

Dame Edith Sitwell, in *The English Eccentrics*, imagined Carlyle's dinner parties in the ground-floor dining-room, 'filled always with a shaggy Highland-cattle-like odour of homespun materials and by a Scotch mist of tobacco smoke.' Dame Edith quoted a letter by Margaret Fuller, the American feminist writer and editor, who had come to Carlyle with an introduction from a fellow sage, Ralph Waldo Emerson:

'I admired [Mr Carlyle's] way of singing his great sentences, so that each one was the stanza of a narrative ballad. . . . He talked of the present state of things in England, giving light, witty sketches of the men of the day, fanatics and others, and some sweet homely stories he told of things he had known of the Scotch peasantry . . . of some poor farmer, or artisan . . . who on Sundays lays aside the cant and care of the dirty English world, and sits . . . looking upon the sea.'

Carlyle could be gruff and overbearing, but he had a gentle heart. He exchanged regular visits with the poet and essayist, Leigh Hunt, who lived in chronic impoverishment at 22 Upper Cheyne Row, a few steps away. When Hunt called on him, Carlyle would leave a guinea on his mantelpiece; unostentatiously, Hunt would pick it up – an unspoken agreement. Despite his insolvency, Hunt was happy in Upper Cheyne Row, a doll's house sort of street. His cramped old-fashioned dwelling reminded him of his childhood: '. . . It had seats in the windows [and] a small room . . . of which I made a *sanctum*, into which no perturbation was to enter . . . there were a few lime trees in front, which in their season diffused a fragrance.'

Other nineteenth-century artists drifted into this evocative corner of London. Dante Gabriel Rossetti came to 16 Cheyne Walk, overlooking the Thames, from Red Lion Square, Holborn, where, with John Millais and William Holman Hunt, he had founded the Pre-Raphaelite Brotherhood. (William Morris and Edward Burne-Jones lived penurious and excitingly Bohemian lives in the same Red Lion Square house.) In Chelsea, Rossetti kept peacocks and a raccoon in his garden. Swinburne shared this abode with him for a while, and so did George Meredith.

James Whistler was their neighbour, at Number 96. During his 12 riverside years Whistler painted his series of shadowy night pieces, the eloquent 'nocturnes' which so enraged the critic Ruskin that he accused the artist of flinging a pot of paint in the public's face. Whistler sued Ruskin over the phrase and was awarded, by a judge with a sense of humour, a farthing in damages.

Whistler's house was daringly decorated for those late Victorian days. He slept in a huge Chinese bed. The dining-room was painted blue and black. Purple Japanese fans were tacked all over the walls and ceilings. His studio was in grey and black, an apt setting for his *Arrangement in Black and White* ('Whistler's Mother'), which hung there along with his portrait of Carlyle. There was also a screen in the studio which he had painted on commission, but had then refused to part with: Battersea Bridge, Chelsea Church and a golden moon against a sky of rich deep blue.

Chelsea continued to shoot off intellectual and artistic fireworks well after World War II, when the annual Chelsea Arts Ball still provoked

43 Rossetti's home at No. 16 Cheyne Walk

audacity and ingenuity. Its local theatre, the Royal Court in Sloane Square, nurtured the 'angry young men' cult, and its English Stage Company exerts a mighty influence on the London theatre. But by the 1960s, the village high street, the King's Road, had undergone a violent change – book shops, antique shops and picture-framers pushed out by the 'swingers', the dimly-lit Carnaby-Street-type boutiques and the *pizzerias*. That too has now ebbed, and Chelsea, once the playground of the muses and then the fairground of the world, is searching for its soul again.

It still has artists, actors, playwrights. (John Osborne has a house in Chelsea Square.) Its pubs buzz with gossip about TV actors, photographers' models and who of what sex is sleeping with whom. But the old guard are only a memory.

Who then was the last of them? Perhaps it was Augustus John, with his curly-brimmed hat, who painted both in Mallord Street and in Wilde's Tite Street (where Sargent also had his studio). Or had the *fin de bohème* truly come some decades earlier, with the passing of lovely Ellen Terry, Henry Irving's leading lady, and possibly the most beautiful ornament the London stage has ever known?

She came to Chelsea when she was 56 and took an ancient house at 215 King's Road – dark brick, standing back from the busy pavement, a bit of garden behind. When it was built more than 250 years ago, Chelsea was still separated from Westminster by the lonely marshlands called the Five Fields, which later became part of Belgravia. The house seems to have had only one previous resident of distinction, Thomas Augustine Arne, who composed *Rule Britannia* as part of a masque written for Frederick Louis, Prince of Wales, the father of George III. Since Dame Ellen's time, however, it has been tenanted by Sir Carol Reed, the film director, and later by Judy Garland.

Ellen Terry cheered the sobriety of the dark panelled rooms with blue curtains and, her grandson, Edward Craig, recalled, with 'bits and pieces that she had picked up while touring the English provincial theatres'. Sir Charles Wheeler, the sculptor and president of the Royal Academy, once saw her entering an open motor car in the King's Road. He was then a young man. She was aging, her bright world already shadowed by the blindness that eventually overtook her:

'She wore a large hat with a veil placed over it . . . and tied beneath the chin.' To him she was still gay, graceful and charming, 'a harmony in grey she might have been painted on canvas by Whistler. But she was real enough, and, equipped against dust and wind, drove off merrily westwards . . . into the golden glow of the setting sun.'

VIII
STAGES AND PLAYERS

ALMOST any evening, not only in central London but in its outlying regions as well, lights go on in 60 or more theatres, opera houses, concert halls, experimental playhouses, pub theatres and, during the summer, outdoor theatres. The range is fantastically wide, from smut to Shakespeare, from pop to Poulenc, from rock musicals to *The Ring*. Nowhere is there such a diversity of live entertainment, nor so high a standard.

Mid-London has three important theatre districts, loosely linked geographically like intersecting circles: the region surrounding Piccadilly Circus with the heaviest concentration in Shaftesbury Avenue and a couple of distinguished strays in the Haymarket; St Martin's Lane with its parallel neighbour, the Charing Cross Road; the Strand, the Aldwych and Covent Garden. But there are a score or more houses of importance, influence and talent outside the West End – the Royal Court in Sloane Square; the Victoria Palace and the Westminster near Victoria Station; the Globe in Southwark; the Mermaid near Blackfriars; Sadler's Wells in Rosebery Avenue, Finsbury; the Palladium, the world's leading variety theatre, near Oxford Circus, and the lovable, draughty Old Vic near Waterloo Station, whose distinguished National Theatre Company transferred early in 1976 to its starkly magnificent new home on the South Bank.

The earliest known fixed theatre was built in 1576 in Shoreditch by an actor, James Burbage. When his lease ran out 21 years later, he dismantled the building, transported it to Bankside and re-erected it as the Globe, the circular theatre where Shakespeare's plays were presented and which he called in *Henry V*, 'this wooden O'.

Shakespeare had a grand-nephew, Charles Hart, who was also

stagestruck, and he became one of the first two stars and the first 'Keeper of the House' or general manager of the Theatre Royal, Drury Lane, the most honoured of all playhouses. In the history of the English drama, there is no place quite like the Lane. The present house, which dates from 1812, is the fourth on the site. Hart's was the first, the King's Theatre, built under a licence granted by Charles II to William Davenant, the poet laureate, and Thomas Killigrew, the royal master of the revels.

Although theatrical entertainments had been under constant harassment from Oliver Cromwell's Puritans, three little companies managed to survive. With the Restoration everything changed. Charles licensed not only Drury Lane, which remained in Killigrew's hands, but granted Davenant the right to build a house of his own, the Duke's Theatre, in Lincoln's Inn Fields. The two were vigorous rivals, outbidding each other for popular performers and successful playwrights. There were times when the Duke's seemed to be winning hands down, but it was Killigrew and Hart, at the head of Charles's 'Company of Comedians', who carved out a unique niche in theatrical history.

And it was to Charles II's most appealing mistress, Nell Gwyn, that Drury Lane owes much of its enduring romantic magnetism. A pub opposite the theatre's main entrance is called Nell of Old Drury. She lived in a slum alley nearby, and as a child served 'strong waters' to the clients at Mother Ross's brothel, in Macklin Street, a few hundred yards north of the present Theatre Royal's stage door.

Her elevation from orange girl to leading player came in part because of her native street-born talent, and in part because she became Charles Hart's mistress when she was 15. Then she took another lover, Lord Charles Buckhurst. When she reached the royal bed in Whitehall Palace, still only 18, she referred jauntily to the king as 'my Charles the Third'. She was a skilled comedienne – Pepys and the public adored her – but shortly after she became the king's mistress, she left the theatre for good.

The first Theatre Royal burned down on the night of 25 January 1672, and nothing but a few scraps of foundation masonry remain deep in the bowels of the present house. Had it lasted into the expansive days of Victorian showbusiness, it would no doubt have been demolished in any case, for it was minute: stage and auditorium together covered only the area occupied by the stage alone today.

His Majesty's Company of Comedians, homeless after the fire, found temporary hospitality in the old Duke's Theatre; by then Davenant's company had left Lincoln's Inn Fields for a new playhouse built by Christopher Wren beside the river in Dorset Gardens near Blackfriars.

44 *above* The Royal Opera House, Covent Garden

The Drury Lane group were deeply in debt. The flames had consumed all their costumes and their properties, leaving as their only asset their inventiveness. Killigrew, irrepressibly optimistic, chose for his opening night a play with the aptest possible title, *Wit Without Money*.

Not to be outdone by Davenant, he too engaged Christopher Wren to build him a new Theatre Royal, under his still existing patent. This proud playhouse was far bigger than the first, occupying approximately the same space as today's. Wren underpinned his structure with sturdy brick arches; in World War II they were used as a bomb shelter. His building lasted 117 years, and was the theatre of David Garrick, Mrs Bracegirdle, Colley Cibber, Perdita Robinson. Garrick became manager in 1747, and began his reign with a prologue written by Dr Johnson, which included the famous line, 'We that live to please must please to live.'

Two decades later there was a new licensee, Richard Brinsley Sheridan, who opened with a revival of a play of his own, *The Rivals*. But he managed the theatre badly. He was no disciplinarian, he hated to delegate authority and schedules baffled him. He began to rehearse his second production even before he had finished writing it, feeding the actors a page or two at a time. It was good – the cast knew that – but rehearsals were so chaotic that Garrick returned to sort things out.

As Sheridan frantically worked on the script in his study upstairs, the prompter, Hopkins, rushed the finished sheets down to the stage. When Sheridan had scrawled the final page, he wrote at its bottom, 'Finished at last. Thank God. RBS.' Hopkins glanced through the closing lines and appended one word, 'Amen'. This was *The School for Scandal*. It opened on 8 May 1777.

The actor who played Sheridan's usurer, Mr Moses, was a former banker, Robert Baddeley. On his death he willed to Drury Lane £100, the interest of which was to provide a cake to be eaten by the current players on every future Twelfth Night. Except for breaks during the two world wars, the Baddeley Cake has always been ceremonially consumed on stage. The cast of one of the Lanes's biggest modern successes, *My Fair Lady*, donated a silver punch bowl and ladle to be used on the occasion.

Among Sheridan's most popular actresses were Sarah Siddons and Dorothy Jordan. The latter attracted the susceptible eye of the Duke of Clarence, and when George III heard that his son was paying her £1,000 a year, he snorted that it was too much and should be halved. The duke passed the dictum along to Mrs Jordan who sent for a Drury Lane playbill and silently pointed to the words printed at the bottom: 'No Money Returned After the Rising of the Curtain'.

George III was frequently at odds with his sons, and he detested even the sight of the Prince of Wales. A memorable row occurred in the rotunda of the Theatre Royal when the two unexpectedly confronted each other. To the shock and surprise (and no doubt delight of some) of the assembled gentry, old George suddenly boxed the ears of young George. The management decided that from then on the antagonists must be kept separate, which is why the Lane is the only theatre in London to have a Prince of Wales's box as well as a monarch's box, and why, over the left entrance to the rotunda, are large incised letters spelling out KING'S SIDE, and above the opposite door, the words, PRINCE'S SIDE.

Today's royal family are more peaceable and, in any case, save on gala occasions, seldom use their boxes. The queen sits in the stalls; Prince Charles prefers the first row of the dress circle. Each of the boxes has a retiring room behind, the prince's tending towards the Regency in decor, the queen's a gem-like little room in pseudo-Adam style, mounting to a miniature dome. When the family are not using

45 Theatre Royal, Haymarket

the boxes, they are for sale, retiring rooms included, to anyone willing to pay only slightly more than the cost of the equivalent number of seats in the stalls. If you have delusions of grandeur, this is the cheapest way in London to indulge them.

Poor Sheridan! Nothing – stars, hit plays, royal patronage – could save him from financial disaster. Wren's old building had by 1791 become badly dilapidated and Sheridan decided to have it torn down. He commissioned Henry Holland to construct a bigger grander house on the old foundations. Costs far exceeded expectations, and the playwright overstretched himself to raise the capital. In 1794 he re-opened with a dramatic triumph, Sarah Siddons as Lady Macbeth. But still the curse of ill luck overhung him.

His career at the Lane ended, however, not with a debtor's whimper, but with the crackle of flames. He was not only playwright and theatre manager, but also one of the most eloquent speakers in the Commons. On the night of 24 February 1809, as he sat in the House, a rosy glow tinted the windows, and a sudden cry went up, 'Fire!' Drury Lane was ablaze and the glare had reflected in the night sky as far away as Westminster. Other members, sympathetic to Sheridan, suggested that the debate be adjourned. There is one story that he thanked them and stayed in his seat, waiting his turn to speak, while his showplace burned to the ground.

A second story seems more characteristic – that he left parliament, went to the Piazza Coffee House in Covent Garden and seated himself beside a window to watch the holocaust, a bottle of port at his elbow. So impassive was he as he surveyed the pyre of all his hopes that a friend remarked on his phlegm. He is said to have replied, 'May not a man be allowed to drink a glass of wine by his own fireside?' One hopes that this version is true.

Destruction was almost complete. A print made after the fire shows what was left: a pillared entrance, a high bulging wall pierced by long arched shattered windows, a half-destroyed column, the ravaged interior. The original royal charter was saved. So were some of Mrs Jordan's costumes and a few of Garrick's wigs. Otherwise, all that remained were Wren's underground arches and an overwhelming load of debt. The theatre, which was worth more than £250,000 had been insured for only £35,000! Sheridan lost his seat in parliament in 1812 and, harried by his creditors, died broken-hearted in 1816, in a borrowed house in Savile Row.

The new Drury Lane, the present house, which was designed by Benjamin Wyatt, had opened on 10 October 1812. It was financed and controlled by a committee assembled by the brewer, Samuel Whitbread.

He had ruthlessly excluded Sheridan, who had yearned for one last chance to recoup his own and the theatre's fortunes but had included among a diverse mix of nobles and businessmen, Lord Byron. Under this committee Londoners for the first time thrilled to the formidable talent of Edmund Kean, who, one critic wrote, 'impressed the audience like a chapter from Genesis'. But the committee ultimately proved a disaster, eternally squabbling, and buying unproducable plays. Byron went through some 500, most of which he had to throw out.

In substance as well as in spirit, the house that saw the rise – and fall, alas – of Edmund Kean is basically unaltered. Every kind of entertainment – drama, opera, pantomime, even cinema – has been seen there. But since the 1920s, it has been renowned chiefly for big musical plays. Ivor Novello, whose own hit shows did much to solidify its supremacy in this genre, called the Lane 'not just a theatre', but 'a tradition, a national treasure'. Postwar, Drury Lane presented a series of the tuneful, fastidiously choreographed American musicals that were then dominating showbusiness – *Oklahoma, Carousel, South Pacific, My Fair Lady, Hello Dolly*.

The Lane has another source of pride – its ghost. Several London theatres also claim to have phantoms, but more people have been ready to swear that they have seen the Lane's, the Man in Grey, than all the others put together. He did not appear until this century, and he never wanders at night. His chief haunt is the upper circle, but once, during World War II, he was encountered backstage in the green room. He is clearly of the eighteenth century, and wears a long grey cloak, high boots, a powdered wig, a tricorn hat and a sword. Members of the audience have noticed him during busy matinees, some assuming him to be a costumed actor. A cleaning woman saw him early one morning during a rehearsal, sitting in the fourth row of the upper circle. When she tried to speak to him, he crossed to the right and vanished through the wall.

The Lane's late biographer, W. J. Macqueen Pope, wrote that he himself saw the apparition on numerous occasions. He offered one theory for its existence: in Victorian times, a workman repairing the side wall of the upper circle broke through the brickwork and found a small room in which lay a skeleton with a dagger in its ribs. Had the murdered man been an actor (which would explain the anachronistic attire), he would undoubtedly have been missed, and the disappearance reported. The coroner held an inquest, but could discover neither identification nor explanation. Mr Pope thought that the bones might have been those of a country gentleman knifed over a love affair with an actress. But of what period? Why should a man in eighteenth-century clothes be bricked up in the wall of an early nineteenth-century theatre, and not start haunting until the twentieth?

The present manager, Mr George Hoare, said to us, 'I myself have never seen him. However, actors sometimes tell me that they have felt a ghostly presence on the stage – a sort of sudden coldness.' Could this be the Man in Grey? For him to venture on to the stage is uncharacteristic. But perhaps after so many years, even a spectre might become stagestruck.

Covent Garden is another of those London areas which are as much a state of mind as a specific place. Its atmosphere pervades eastward beyond Drury Lane, westward to Bedford Street and southward past the little world of publishing around Maiden Lane and Southampton Street, into the Strand. But what is Covent Garden itself? Until 1975 it was London's central fruit, flower and vegetable market – Shaw's setting for the opening scene of *Pygmalion*. Now the suppliers have moved south of the river.

It would be foolish to deny that something romantic, precious and lively has gone with them – and not only the all-night pubs where early-to-rise market man and late-to-bed party-goers used to mingle. True, cabbage leaves and turnip greens no longer litter the pavements; nor do yesterday's bulky provision lorries any more block Russell Street, Floral Street, Henrietta Street, Mart Street and the open space before St Paul's church. Yet there was a rhythm, a harmony to it all. Listen to what Oscar Wilde had to say about the market as it was at dawn:

> 'Huge carts filled with nodding lilies rumbled slowly down the polished empty street. The air was heavy with the perfume of the flowers. . . . A long line of boys carrying crates of striped tulips and of yellow and red irises [threaded] their way through the huge jade-green piles of vegetables. . . . The heavy cart-horses slipped and stamped upon the rough stones, shaking their bells and trappings. Some of the drivers were lying asleep on a pile of sacks. Iris-necked and pink-footed the pigeons ran about picking up seeds.'

Covent Garden was originally a convent garden, the property of the monks of Westminster Abbey. After the Reformation, the site – about seven acres – became the property of the Bedford family, and somewhere along the way the 'n' in convent dropped out. The Bedfords built their London house in the southern portion, fronting the Strand. The fourth earl established the open piazza, possibly in imitation of the Place Royale (now the Place des Vosges) in Paris, which Henri IV had laid out 20 years earlier.

The earl created arcaded buildings along the north and east sides of the square; these arches themselves later came to be called 'piazzas'. To fill the west side, he turned to Inigo Jones. What he wanted there was a church, but not a costly one: 'I would not have it much better than a barn.' Jones replied, 'You shall have, my lord, the handsomest barn in England.' And there it stands, St Paul's, with a columned portico and a heavy, stately pediment whose eaves extend well beyond the width of the porch. The effect is not Christian but pagan: St Paul's is a northern sister of the Parthenon.

At the square's north-east corner is Covent Garden's second historic theatre, the Royal Opera House. There are perhaps six or seven truly top-level opera houses in the world. Leaving aside the eccentric new wind-blown one in Sydney, which has yet to win its artistic laurels, they include La Scala in Milan, the Paris Opera, New York's Metropolitan, the Vienna, possibly the Hamburg and, of course, Covent Garden. Of them all, Covent Garden ranks highest with performers and audiences alike. Mr John Tooley, the general administrator, commented, 'A success for a new singer here makes impresarios everywhere sit up and take notice.'

Covent Garden's progenitor, John Rich, had in the 1720s inherited from his father control of Davenant's old theatre in Lincoln Inn's Fields, and, more important, Charles II's patent. With this in his pocket, he decided to build a new house. Although structurally it was modelled on the Opera House in the Haymarket (not the predecessor of the present Haymarket Theatre, but of another, long gone, on the opposite side of the road), Rich did not intend it as a home for *dramma per musica*. He wanted directly to challenge Drury Lane, and chose to build near the premier theatre, on a site opening out into one of Bedford's piazzas.

Even in a profession so peopled with oddities as the theatre, John Rich cut a grotesque figure – an illiterate who owned 27 cats and was a skilled pantomimist.

He opened his playhouse in 1732 with a revival of Congreve's *Way of the World* which was more than 30 years old; the first night half the seats were empty. It took another revival, *The Beggar's Opera*, which Rich himself had launched four years earlier with colossal success in Lincoln's Inn Fields, to get his new venture going. Two years later he began a long association with music, producing seven of Handel's operas, some to profit and acclaim, others to poor houses. The German composer turned to writing oratorios, and Rich presented these in 'sacred concerts' during Lent for a number of years. But to earn his keep, he returned to drama, notably to Shakespeare and to Restoration plays. Garrick acted at Covent Garden for a season before taking over Drury Lane.

Rich died in 1761 and his theatre passed to his two sons-in-law. One, John Beard, was a distinguished tenor for whom Mozart had written several roles, and he tried again to stage opera. But as before, the attempt failed, and for several decades plays were once more the theatre's mainstay, especially those of Sheridan and Goldsmith. Mrs Siddons acted there in the 1780s, and in 1803, her brother, John Philip Kemble became the manager, mounting Shakespeare in profusion, and presenting Grimaldi, the immortal clown, in *Mother Goose*.

In 1808, fire swept the building. It was thought to have started when a piece of wadding shot from a property gun was left to smoulder unnoticed and finally ignited some backstage draperies. Everything was consumed, including Handel's organ; 25 people died trying to stem the blaze. There is an irony to the story: the production that night was *Pizarro* by Sheridan, whose own theatre had less than a year to stand before it too burned to the ground.

One of Covent Garden's biographers, Desmond Shawe-Taylor, meditating on the frequency of London's theatrical fires, wonders not that there should have been so many, but that there were not even more. Wood-framed scenery, fabric drops and transparencies and candles, candles, candles everywhere – it is amazing that there have been only four Drury Lanes and three Covent Gardens. What is even more astonishing is the speed with which new theatres sprang up, as if cued into sudden life by some master prompter.

Rich's house was replaced within a twelvemonth by one of the largest in Europe, some 500 seats more than the first, and considerably more capacious than the present Royal Opera. Like today's, its entrance fronted on Bow Street, and a stately entrance it was, screened by a four-pillared porch recalling the Temple of Pallas Athene, with bas-reliefs and neo-classical statues. Of the three Covent Gardens, the second was externally by far the most attractive.

The staff was enormous: choristers, musicians, dancers, painters, colour-grinders, carpenters, stagehands, firemen, porters and numerous executives to oversee the multiplicity of departments. All this was costly, so up went the price of tickets. It is amusing to compare the current fatalistic acceptance of inflationary rises with what happened on 18 September 1809. The public had bought their tickets for *Macbeth*, the play which all actors believe is accursed, and filed quietly inside. But when the curtain rose, they broke into the most stupendous riot in theatre history. The entire audience began to shout, 'Old Prices!' or, more simply, 'O.P.', stamping on the floor or thumping with sticks in perfect rhythm. The din make Shakespeare's words inaudible.

It was the same on the second night. On the third, Kemble faced the rioters and asked what they wanted. As though he didn't know! They replied by tossing handbills and coins on to the stage, all carrying the message, 'O.P.' Ill-advisedly, Kemble hired professional prize fighters to quell the mob, but this made matters worse, and the pandemonium went on night after night for two months. At last Kemble's resistance crumbled. He cut the prices back and apologized to the audience for his strong-arm squad. They lifted a sign which read, 'We are satisfied' and the O.P. riots were over.

During its first ten years the new theatre wavered between periods of numbing failure and stunning success, between drama and musical drama. One of its strangest evenings was that of 20 May 1817. Mozart's *Don Giovanni* had been cheered and applauded at the Haymarket Opera the previous month, and Kemble promptly stole it, had it rewritten in English, retitled it *The Libertine* and announced it as 'the interesting story of Don Juan in which will be introduced the celebrated music of Mozart's *Don Giovanni*'. Kemble's brother, Charles, played the great lover, but apparently no one was confident enough of this pastiche to let it stand on its own. *Hamlet* was performed on the same bill, and every time Kemble showed *The Libertine* afterwards, he also showed another full-length play.

By the end of the decade, both Mrs Siddons and her brother had retired, and Charles Kemble became co-manager. From then on the swing was more and more towards grand opera – Weber, Rossini, Donizetti, Mozart and two operas, *I Due Foscari* and *Ernani*, by a young composer scarcely known to London audiences, Giuseppe Verdi. Towards mid-century the theatre was rebuilt 'along Italian lines' and in 1847 it was proclaimed a full-fledged opera house, henceforth to be known as The Royal Italian Opera, Covent Garden. In the first season there were 17 productions, and 19 in the second, plus 11 more sung in English!

Between operatic seasons, the management let the theatre out for other entertainments, and in December 1855, they signed a fateful lease. They turned it over for ten weeks to John Henry Anderson, a showman who promoted himself as 'The Wizard of the North', and presented a weird farrago of drama, spectacle and farce. He climaxed his tenure on 4 March 1856 with a masked ball, undoubtedly the most gruesome event in the theatre's history. A *London Journal* writer described it as 'a monstrous leprosy, a sickening picture . . . of human degradation and vice [at which] the women were disgustingly attired, flaunting their scarcely disguised figures in the glare of satanic revelry. . . . The males were a mass of demonry – thieves, gamblers, roués . . . disciples of the lewd fiend, Belial.' As for the entertainment, 'the vilest ballet ever put on the vilest stage in Europe was modest in comparison . . . the dancing girls of the East were angels of purity compared with these soul-and-body lost parodies of their sex.'

Not since Biblical times has unseemly revelry been so promptly rebuked. Just before five a.m. the roof burst into flames. Screaming, the merry-makers fought their way out into Bow Street. In less than 30 minutes the roof had crashed to the floor, and by first light all was gone: the theatre, four Hogarth paintings, the entire library including the original manuscript of *The School for Scandal* (fire and Sheridan once more!) and settings, costumes and properties for 60 operas.

To the management it was a morning of ebony gloom. Any time-traveller from the 1970s would probably have been hooted back to his own century if he had dared to tell them that Covent Garden's greatest days still lay ahead, and would stretch far into the impenetrable future.

The building which replaced the old one – today's – was designed by E. M. Barry (the son of parliament's architect) and opened in 1858. Aristocratic in line, luxurious in mood, a thoroughbred from the richest of all periods of theatrical construction, the Victorian, it was to house some of the most glorious singers and some of the most brilliant productions that musical history can show, bridging the generations from Gounod to Benjamin Britten and from Grisi, Patti and the De Reszke brothers through Melchior and Flagstad to Maria Callas, Geraint Evans, Joan Sutherland, Jussi Björling and Beverly Sills.

The tradition that opera was an Italian art had lasted until 1891. By then, with operas in French and German taking up more and more of the repertory, the name 'Royal Italian Opera' became a misleading fiction, and the word 'Italian' was dropped. Stars came to Covent Garden from every musical firmament. Nellie Melba arrived from Australia to become the audience's darling, and, in 1902, heralded by her enthusiastic reports, Enrico Caruso appeared in London. One can only envy the opera-goers of that season, for they saw what must surely have been the most stirring *Bohème* of all time, with Melba as Mimi and Caruso as Rodolfo.

During the two world wars the music had to stop. In the first, the graceful, horseshoe-shaped auditorium became a furniture warehouse; in the second, it was a dance hall for Allied troops. In 1946 it re-opened triumphantly, not only as a home for opera, but also for the best in ballet. To Covent Garden came Ninette de Valois and her renowned Sadler's Wells company, bringing with her the conductor, Constant Lambert. Now called the Royal Ballet, the company has soared to even greater heights with such creative choreographers (besides de Valois herself) as Frederick Ashton, Robert Helpmann, Kenneth MacMillan and John Cranko; such superb dancers as Antoinette Sibley, Merle Park, Margot Fonteyn and Rudolf Nureyev; such imaginative designers as Cecil Beaton, John Piper and Oliver Messel.

The first post-war production, a shimmeringly beautiful *Sleeping Beauty*, was performed before King George VI and Queen Elizabeth. In those days of austerity, with bomb ruins littering London and the streets still partly blacked out, the glow under the saucer-shaped turquoise ceiling was itself heartwarming – sconces casting warm red light on the gold and ivory tiers and on the rich burgundy walls. That night the king and queen, the princesses and Queen Mary sat in the royal box, the second from the stage in the grand tier on the audience's right.

On evenings of state now, a temporary box is set up for Queen Elizabeth II and her party in the centre of the grand tier – the better both to see and be seen. But the old royal box has atmosphere. The gold chairs made for Victoria and Albert are still there. So is a settee against one wall, facing *away* from the stage. Here, out of sight, sat Victoria's ladies-in-waiting. But the queen had a twinge of conscience, and ordered a mirror placed on the opposite wall so that they could see the production in reflection. The mirror is still there too.

Covent Garden is the only theatre in the western world which maintains both a full-time grand opera company and a full-time ballet company. Between them, they keep the theatre alight for 45 or 46 weeks a year, far longer than most.

If, of London's three foremost historic theatres Drury Lane is the deepest-rooted and Covent Garden the grandest, the Haymarket is by far the most stylish – small, almost feminine. The auditorium's dominant colours are rich blue and soft glowing gold – not gold paint, but genuine gold leaf. And above the proscenium is the most exquisitely executed royal arms in all of England.

Externally the Haymarket presents a row of columns and a Grecian pediment facing westward towards St James's Square along Charles II Street. The best view of the theatre – the one its architect, John Nash, had in mind – is from the square. The classic façade fills the entire vista much as the Madeleine completes with perfect harmony the end of the Rue Royale as seen from the Place de la Concorde. By night, with the Haymarket floodlit, the spectacle is the quintessence of old-fashioned metropolitan glamour. So much beauty in a street which began life as a public way in which carts loaded with hay and straw were permitted free of toll!

Backstage the Haymarket remains much as Nash intended. The most home-like, the most liveable dressing rooms in London, say actors, who until a few years ago used to sit comfortably awaiting their calls in front of dainty Regency fireplaces. Fire regulations made it necessary to block them, but the pretty mantels are still there.

This house was preceded by the Little Theatre in the Hay, built in 1720 on a site beside the present one, where a rough old country pub had stood, in which corn buyers and sellers used to haggle. Only the King's and the Duke's Theatres then held royal patents to perform drama, and the little house in the Hay operated sometimes with temporary licences, sometimes outside the law, using such subterfuges as selling tickets for a concert and offering *free of charge* in addition a 'rehearsal' of, say, *Romeo and Juliet*.

There was a whiff of rebellion about the place: in 1737, Henry Fielding was managing it, and he presented one play, *The Historical Register*, which poked such shameless and vituperative fun at Sir Robert Walpole that the prime minister, in retaliation, had an act rushed through parliament making it mandatory for all plays to be approved by the lord chamberlain before they could be performed. This censorship lasted 231 years, 'protecting' the British public from such unseemly spectacles as actors portraying recent or incumbent monarchs or, for that matter, God or His Son. Thus, prior to 1968 when the act was repealed, and thanks to the cheekiness of the Theatre in the Hay, such productions as *Jesus Christ Superstar*, *Godspell* and *Crown Matrimonial* (which opened at the Haymarket) would have been denied to English theatre-goers.

In 1767, after a series of entertainments so mild as to be innocuous, the Haymarket became a Theatre Royal, and in 1821 it was replaced by Nash's building. It was soon the most prestigious house in London for drama and comedy, and in modern times the setting for every sort of play from Wilde to Ibsen, from Barrie to T. S. Eliot, from Maugham to Rattigan, from Coward to Tennessee Williams.

The most recent managers have been the Watson family – father, son and mother. Mrs Sylva Stuart Watson is an enthusiastic octogenarian who began her professional life as a singer. We talked with her in her Regency office, part wood-panelled, part damask-lined and heavily overlaid with theatrical prints. Mrs Watson's attitude towards the Haymarket is loving, protective and conservative. She has two rules: she will not permit 'blue' plays and she insists that *God Save the Queen* must be played at every performance, making the Haymarket the sole adherent to a custom which was once universal.

Only very big cities produce streets like St Martin's Lane. A mere 250 yards long, it is an animated amiable confusion – three major live theatres and one for films, a county court, restaurants, pubs, bookshops. Lanes and alleys open off it in both directions, and in these are shops which sell dancing shoes, old prints, antiques, wigs, masks and more food and drink. One byway to the east, Godwin's Court, a row of seventeenth-century brick houses with bow windows, is thought to be the oldest street in London. Those to the west link St Martin's Lane by way of stage doors with the Charing Cross Road, where two more theatres stand. The two streets join forces at the bottom and debouche past the statue of Nurse Edith Cavell and the National Portrait Gallery into Trafalgar Square.

At night, standing in the square and looking beyond the floodlit columns of the National Gallery and of St Martin-in-the-Fields, your eye is drawn upwards, where St Martin's Lane itself begins, to a large glimmering globe high in the sky which seems to be revolving. This tops London's largest theatre, the Coliseum.

Edward VII was on the throne when Oswald Stoll, an enterprising empire-builder of 35, who already owned a string of music halls, decided to create a palace for variety within easy reach of the new Charing Cross Station, where commuters come in. He conceived a colossal showpiece, an auditorium with 2,350-odd seats and the solid opulence of the old Cunard liners – marble and alabaster, mahogany and bronze. On the technical side he was equally openhanded; his stage incorporates three concentric revolves, the first ever seen in England, which can rotate independently at speeds up to 20 miles an hour. Once he staged a race, with three horses running against the direction of the turn-tables.

He and his mother, who often sat in the box-office selling tickets, and whose marble bust now stands in the lobby, were in one way precursors of the Haymarket's Mrs Watson: blue jokes by a performer meant instant dismissal. Otherwise, anything went. Stoll mounted rodeos, tennis matches and naval battles. He commissioned short plays from Bernard Shaw and J. M. Barrie. He engaged the greatest names of the day – Sarah Bernhardt, Mrs Patrick Campbell, Ellen Terry, Diaghilev's Russian ballet. He hired a child actor, Master Noël Coward.

But variety in Britain, like vaudeville in the United States, faltered and virtually died in the years between the wars. The Coliseum shifted to spectacular operettas, the most elaborate of which was *White Horse Inn*. After World War II, like Drury Lane, it staged a series of big, brassy American musicals – *Annie Get Your Gun*, *Kiss Me Kate*, *Guys and Dolls*.

Since 1968, it has been the home of the English National Opera, which was known until 1974 as the Sadler's Wells Opera. Productions are in English, and vocally and technically, compare favourably with those at Covent Garden. Some of the leading singers appear with both companies. Because the English National Opera does not present ballets as well, its operatic programme is considerably larger than Covent Garden's – some 25 productions a year.

And now to the newest jewel in London's theatrical diadem, the National Theatre, which opened in March 1976. Directly across the Thames from Somerset House, it is part of a gradually developing arts complex on the South Bank, including the Royal Festival Hall, the Queen Elizabeth Hall, the Purcell Room, the National Film Theatre and the Hayward Gallery.

The South Bank was a mixture of slum, run-down light industry and warehousing until much of the region was cleared for the Festival of Britain in 1951. The cultural institutions which now cluster there are still not spiritually a part of London, perhaps because the massive block-like architecture and the drabness of the adjacent streets create a brooding mood, barren, faintly hostile. Should this opinion seem negative, it is fair to say that the National Theatre building and its neighbours achieve, through their very size and the uncompromising harshness of their silhouettes, a species of grandeur. If the entire development stood in the midst of the Sahara, one could well imagine that it had been devised to propitiate some ill-tempered deity.

A National Theatre Company – as distinct from a theatre building – was started in 1962 under the leadership of Sir Laurence (later Lord) Olivier at the Old Vic in the Waterloo Road – officially, The Victoria. This little playhouse was, in the days of its royal namesake, the home of melodrama and known to its regulars as 'the Bucket of Blood'. In later years, two indomitable women, Emma Cons and Lilian Bayliss, transformed it into a people's palace for classic plays, especially Shakespeare's. Miss Bayliss, who ran it for 25 years, was also the moving force behind the Sadler's Wells opera and ballet companies. Legend has entwined 'the lady', as her intimates called her, with tendrils of anecdote. She was profoundly religious and sought divine guidance in all her managerial problems. If an actor requested a rise, she would return to her office, fall upon her knees and put the matter to her maker. Usually, neither Miss Bayliss nor Jehovah could spare the cash. She is the godmother of the new National Theatre.

In 1973, when construction was nearing completion, Lord Olivier retired because of ill health, and Peter Hall, who had in 1960 created the Royal Shakespeare Company, became its director.

In no traditional sense is the monumental National, designed by Denis Lasdun, a theatre. It has no lighted front, no suggestion of gilt, plush, cherubs or showbiz glitter. Its lobbies and bars are temple-like, with open spaces juxtaposed dramatically on varying levels, and with unexpected, startlingly beautiful views of the river. There is an Aeschylean austerity, a vastness in which the ordering of a gin-and-tonic seems almost heresy. The very barmaids, one feels, should be wearing tragic masks and Grecian robes.

The National is, however, a superb theatre-*machine*, and contains not one playhouse, but three. The Lyttelton, the first to open, in March 1976, comes closest to the conventional, with a curtain and a proscenium. The Olivier, largest of the trio, is an amphitheatre, steeply raked like those of ancient Attica. The Cottesloe is a small box for experimental productions.

The Lyttelton is a sombre auditorium seating 890, with dazzlingly advanced backstage equipment and a versatile proscenium which can expand or contract both vertically and horizontally. When we saw Ibsen's *John Gabriel Borkman* there, the proscenium's value was immediately apparent: the interiors in the first three acts were tightly enclosed, but in the last, the scene, a barren snowy hillside, filled almost the entire stage, with the proscenium's top and sides drawn back to their fullest dimensions, to provide an enormous stage picture.

The opening of the Olivier (1,160 seats) some half a year later was, however, the shining event, culminative and overwhelming. The play was Christopher Marlowe's *Tamburlaine*, a dense texture of blood, violence, fire and conquest, related in wild and whirling words. Stunning though the production was, the theatre itself was the star of the evening. 'The most imposing, pre-eminent in the land,' wrote Milton Shulman of *The Evening Standard*. The stage, three-quarters encircled by tier above tier of spectators, said Irving Wardle of *The Times*, enabled the actor 'to hold the entire audience in his fist'.

The only pity was that Peter Hall had had to reach back four centuries to find a play worthy of it. The Olivier cries out for the classic dramatists of tomorrow, for a new Marlowe, another Shakespeare, a Shaw capable of even more than *Saint Joan* or *Caesar and Cleopatra*.

The public reaction to the National's external architecture ranged

46 Foyer of the Lyttelton Theatre, part
of the South Bank National Theatre block

47 *left* The Coliseum, St Martin's Lane

from outrage and derogation to extravagant praise. Regardless of one's own feelings about its rough concrete walls, no one can disagree with what Harold Hobson, the dean of London critics, wrote of the company itself – that it would be difficult to rival anywhere. An ensemble that can call upon such talents as those of Dame Peggy Ashcroft, Wendy Hiller, Sir Ralph Richardson, Sir John Gielgud, Albert Finney, Roland Culver, Frank Finlay and Angela Lansbury among others, must surely represent a peak of acting prowess unknown since the days of Sir Henry Irving and Dame Ellen Terry.

The National cannot help but become the unchallenged epicentre of the entire seething seismic world of the international theatre.

IX

A BED FOR THE NIGHT

When Jane Austen visited London from her Hampshire village, she usually stayed with her brother Henry, in Sloane Street. In the eighteenth century the gently-born always chose to lodge with friends and relations; the public inn was far too coarse. There was then only one respectable 'family' hotel in London. It had been established in 1774 in a Covent Garden mansion built more than a century earlier (probably by Inigo Jones) which had been Thomas Killigrew's home when he managed Drury Lane. In 1790, it was taken over by W. C. Evans, who christened it Evans's Hotel and Supper Rooms; his name clung through many changes of hands and several guises – coffee house, music hall, tavern. For a time in recent years it was a fruit warehouse. It still stands at 43 King Street, newly restored, stately as ever, the handsomest building in the Garden.

Since Evans's day hotels in London have proliferated. Some splendid ones, redolent of the *fin de siècle*, have disappeared: Hitler destroyed the Carlton, where once Escoffier ruled; the aristocratic Cecil was replaced by an office block; the lavish Langham with its winter garden is now a workaday adjunct of the BBC. Skyscraper hotels have burgeoned, many of them members of international chains, efficient, impersonal, not entirely endearing. Some will no doubt develop style, but like patina on furniture, this takes time and care.

We have chosen to write of only a few of London's most distinguished hotels – what the Italians call so resonantly *i grandi alberghi* – those with the longest or the richest histories, those whose standards never falter. The first was begun in two adjoining houses in Brook Street by a French chef, Jacques Mivart, in 1815, the year of Waterloo, and it eventually became Claridge's. A couple of other French chefs,

48 The entrance hall at Claridge's

Alexander Grillion and Jean Escudier, had by then already set up as hoteliers in Mayfair, and were firmly implanting the tradition that it was in this *quartier* that visiting royalty were housed. Roly-poly Louis XVIII stopped with Grillion for three nights on his way back to Paris to reclaim the throne his family had lost in the Revolution; a future queen of England, Princess Adelaide of Saxe-Meiningen, stayed at Grillion's, before her marriage to the Duke of Clarence. Escudier played host to the Grand Duchess Catherine of Russia.

But it was Mivart's Hotel, above all, which became known as 'the usual residence of sovereign princes'. Its reputation as a sort of annexe to Buckingham Palace continued after Mivart sold out in 1838 to a former butler, William Claridge, the first Englishman to become world-famous as a hotel-keeper. (James Brown, who had been a butler to Lord Byron, started his long-lived Brown's Hotel in Dover Street a little later.) Claridge and his wife, who had worked with him as house-keeper for a number of important families, had been running a small hotel next door to Mivart's, and when he put the two together, he continued to use the Frenchman's name, for it was by far the better known. Even when he displayed his own, he still prudently added, 'late Mivart's'.

In 1860, the Empress Eugénie stayed there. On 11 December, Queen Victoria wrote to her Uncle Leopold, King of the Belgians, 'We . . . visited [the empress] at Claridge's Hotel.' From that moment, Claridge's was, as Karl Baedeker called it a few years later, 'the first hotel in London'.

William Claridge sold the hotel in 1880, for £60,000. Over the next decade and a half, his triumph grew shabby and old-fashioned. New ideas were approaching from across the Atlantic – lifts, or 'ascending rooms' as they were called, central heating, floor service, electric lighting, private baths, telephones. In 1889, Richard D'Oyly Carte opened his glittering new Savoy Hotel in the Strand, and six years later the Savoy Group bought Claridge's, pulled down the little houses and constructed the building we know today, at the corner of Brook Street and Davies Street.

Compared with the Savoy, it was still extremely modest, faced with Mayfair's typical turn-of-the-century red brick and hinting at its internal lustre only through its top-hatted doorman and the range of flagstaffs above its entrance. It had all – or almost all – the modern refinements that D'Oyly Carte's flagship, the Savoy, boasted. The management, fearing the effect of the innovations upon old-established clients, assured them that the changes would not 'interfere with their comfort and privacy'.

So far as the dawning of a more strident century permitted, this was no empty promise. Claridge's scorns publicity, never reveals the names of its guests and avoids dance bands and cabaret. It does not even call itself Claridge's Hotel – only Claridge's. Nor does it advertise its prices; what a client pays is regarded as a purely private matter.

Truman Capote's Holly Golightly said that Tiffany's 'calms me down right away, the calmness and the proud look of it; nothing very bad could happen to you there.' She would have felt the same if she had ever entered Claridge's. A wood fire crackles in the entrance lobby, a statuesque wrought-iron staircase curves upward, flower arrangements glow in wall niches, liveried footmen move softly across thick carpets in drawing-rooms that might have been whisked out of a stately home. No, nothing bad could ever happen in Claridge's – except perhaps that confidential bill.

The hotel can cope grandly with more than a single monarch at a time. It has one particularly luxurious royal suite which includes a sunken marble bath and a manorial dining-room; there are several other suites only a touch less regal. Once, when two kings wanted *the* suite at the same time, the management diplomatically told them both that the ceiling was undergoing repair, and accommodated each of them in the fractionally less lush apartments, neither better by one degree than the other.

During World War II, King George II, exiled from Greece, lived in the hotel incognito for five years as 'Mr Brown', a sad, gaunt, lonely figure. In the same period, Claridge's sheltered Wilhelmina, Queen of the Netherlands, King Haakon of Norway, King Peter of Yugoslavia, the Grand Duchess Charlotte of Luxembourg, the President of Poland and Princess Alexandra, daughter of Princess Aspasia of the Hellenes. In 1944, Claridge's was the setting for a royal romance when King Peter and Princess Alexandra drove off in a car borrowed from King George VI for their austerity wartime wedding. Their first child, the crown prince, was born in the hotel about a year later. At the wedding of the present Queen Elizabeth, so many crowned heads stopped at the hotel that, when someone telephoned and asked, 'May I speak to the king, please?' the switchboard operator could reply only, 'Which king?'

One can well fancy that the 'boots' in Claridge's would have many a fascinating tale to tell – if he were not so discreet. It is impossible to picture glamour, comedy or tragedy associated with one of those do-it-yourself shoe-buffers that you find in the upstairs corridors of so many modern hotels. Sam Weller was a boots at the White Hart in Southwark when he met his future master, Mr Pickwick. He classified

49 The Dorchester, Park Lane

his clients by their footwear: 'Who is there in the house? There's a vooden leg in number six, there's a pair of Hessians in thirteen, there's two pair of halves in the commercial, there's these here painted tops in the snuggery inside the bar, and five more tops in the coffee room. . . . Stop a bit. . . . Yes; there's a pair of Vellingtons a good deal vorn, and a pair o' lady's shoes, in number five.'

Recent construction does not necessarily mean 'modernity'. The supreme example of how to maintain old standards in a new building, even a new location, is the Berkeley in Wilton Place, Knightsbridge, which opened in 1972. So determinedly does the Berkeley cling to fading ways, its manager told us, that clients who have been heavily indoctrinated in the customs of international chains must often be gently nudged into using the services available, encouraged to put their shoes in the corridor at night, to ring for the maid or the valet.

The old Berkeley used to stand almost opposite the Ritz in Piccadilly, and was descended from a coaching inn, the Gloucester Coffee House and Hotel. It attained its fame in the 1920s, when debutantes, their sharp-eyed mammas and the Bright Young Things, that floating society of slightly scandalous and much-gilded youth, took it up. In the daring days of bobbed hair, short skirts and imported jazz, the Berkeley *was* the contemporary scene. One associates it with names like Noël Coward, Gertrude Lawrence, Michael Arlen and their fashionable admirers.

By the 1970s, however, what remained of high society had almost totally shifted from Mayfair and St James's westward to Knightsbridge, Belgravia and Chelsea, with Sloane Street, once a neighbourly avenue of grocers, fishmongers and a scattering of antique, art, millinery and dress shops, transmuted into a more avant-garde and glossier Bond Street. The management of the Berkeley decided to move with the trend. To avoid too harsh a rupture, parts of the old hotel were re-installed in the new – the entire writing room designed by Edwin Lutyens, wall panelling, marble fireplaces, chandeliers, bedroom furniture, even light brackets.

The hotel soon received an approving royal nod. Not long after it opened, a gentleman telephoned to reserve a secluded table in the restaurant for himself and two ladies, 'one of whom you will recognize'. This turned out to be the queen. An American who was lunching alone while his wife nursed a headache upstairs, cast an incredulous look at her majesty, rushed to the house phone and called his wife: "You've got to come down right away! No matter how rotten you feel, this is one lunch you can't miss!'

No street has been changed more by hotel-building over the past 40-odd years than Park Lane. The transformation began in the financially bleak days of the 'twenties and 'thirties, when great town houses became impossibly costly to run. The mighty walls of one after another began to crumble as the wreckers' ball thundered against them. Others have been demolished since, and Grosvenor House, the Dorchester, the Hilton, the Inn on the Park, the Londonderry and the Intercontinental have taken their places.

All have their newsworthy clientele, from Arab sheiks to admen, best-selling novelists to business moguls. But it is undoubtedly the Dorchester, roughly midway between Hyde Park Corner and Marble Arch, which wins the laurels for sheer splashiness. Its Oliver Messel suite, a gardened penthouse, has probably housed more film stars than any other set of rooms in London. The hotel is restrainedly art-deco on the outside, pillared and arabesqued in the eighteenth-century manner on the inside. Its floors are sound-proofed with seaweed.

Old Dorchester House which was torn down in 1929 to make way for it was a Renaissance-style palazzo built by a Victorian millionaire, R. S. Holford, on the spot where, much earlier, the Earls of Dorchester had lived. Holford's son, George, became an equerry to Edward VII, and his house, at the peak of its fame, was the most fashionable social centre in London. The Shah of Persia rented it in 1895. A few years later the American ambassador, Whitelaw Reid, took it over as his residence, at an annual rent of 4,500 guineas; over the front door he mounted a gigantic marble eagle that he had found in Rome. His countrymen at home criticized him as extravagant, but their self-righteousness backfired when they learned that he was paying the rent from his own pocket.

Only one thing from Holford's mansion is preserved in the hotel – some wood panelling installed in an upstairs corridor. But something less tangible and far more characteristic has also lingered on: party-giving on a grand scale. The Dorchester, unlike the Berkeley and Claridge's, is a flaunting peacock!

Among the most spectacular parties in recent years were three given by heads of state during official visits. In each case, the queen was the guest of honour. King Hussein of Jordan gave a luncheon in the ball-room which the Dorchester's resident decorator, Oliver Ford, transformed into a tropical garden, with a flower-banked pool 65 feet long where water lilies floated and goldfish swam. The walls were draped with green and white silk, against which stood tall pyramids of white carnations.

For the late King Feisal of Saudia Arabia, Mr Ford swathed the room in curtains of green and red – Saudi Arabia's national colours – and the royal guests sat under an Arabian Nights canopy of cloth-of-gold upon white silk chairs embroidered with their coats-of-arms.

Undoubtedly the most vulgar party of all (the hostess ordained that it *must* be vulgar) was the extravaganza Elizabeth Taylor staged for Richard Burton's 50th birthday. Two hundred yards of gold lamé were made up as tablecloths and curtains. Food was set out on coster-mongers' barrows hung with red and gold balloons. The guests helped themselves to dressed crab, smoked salmon, turkey, ham, tongue, beef Stroganoff, curried chicken, baked potatoes wrapped in gold foil, sausages and mash and tripe and onions – the last two, Burton's favourite dishes. They sat on gold chairs, ate by the light of gold candles in holders made of gold leaves and danced on a floor sprayed with gold paint.

With so many superlatives heaped by so many demanding clients on the hotels we've already discussed, it seems impossible that there should be one which exceeds them all in the minds of thousands of discerning globe-trotters. But among the cognoscenti, the Savoy is regularly referred to as '*the* best hotel in the world'. For the completeness of its service and the variety of its skills, there is no hotel anywhere that rivals it.

'Whenever Marlene Dietrich stays here, she sleeps in my bed', Claudio Buttafava, the ebullient reception manager told us. He was not confiding any indiscretion, simply explaining that Miss Dietrich likes an over-sized bed. Mr Buttafava's is the largest in the hotel. So it is moved into her suite, and he tucks up in his own room on a standard-sized mattress.

An American magnate from the Far West refuses to acknowledge that crossing the time zones both of the States and of the Atlantic Ocean puts him hours ahead. He goes on operating according to his usual 'tummy time', and for as long as he stays in the Savoy, even if it's several months, a full dinner is served to him at about three a.m., GMT. Providing complete meals at any hour of the day or night is taken for granted. Mr Beverley Griffin, the general manager, said to us, 'Why shouldn't a civilized man eat when he wants to, and not when other people think he ought?'

The more eccentric a request, the better the Savoy seems to like it. In the central reservation office, 120,000 file cards list the quirks and needs of all regular clients. (The Berkeley, Claridge's and the Connaught maintain similar records, but none is quite so exhaustive.) Notes are jotted by the head housekeeper, the superintendent of floor waiters and the management: No pink flowers in Mrs A's room. She threw them out the window last time. . . . Countess B can't sleep with patterned curtains. Insists upon stripes. . . . Sheik C's bed must be positioned so that he lies facing Mecca. . . . Salt with melon, hot milk with corn flakes, oysters for breakfast – if you have ever revealed an idiosyncracy, the Savoy has recorded it!

Never was a guest more precise in his desires than the late Noël Coward. Said Mr Griffin, 'The Master wanted five pillows and a large bed. He wanted the tables, the chairs, his pills, his water glass all in exactly the same place every time. When we got the arrangement absolutely the way he liked it, we had it photographed.' From then on, the housekeeper followed the picture in detail.

The Savoy occupies a sharply sloping site between the Strand and the Thames where, in the thirteenth century, Count Peter of Savoy built for himself 'the fayrest mannor in Europe'. Over the hotel's Strand entrance, a bronze-gilt statue of Peter, shield on arm and spear poised high, welcomes the visitor. Peter's niece, Eleanor of Provence,

had married the Plantagenct monarch, Henry III, and the king rented Peter the tract in exchange for 'three barbed arrows' a year. Into his palace Peter imported many 'beautiful foreign ladies' whom he married off to English noblemen.

Later the palace was occupied by Simon de Montfort, founder of the House of Commons, and afterwards by John of Gaunt, Duke of Lancaster, who often entertained Geoffrey Chaucer at dinner. The building was eventually destroyed and replaced by a hospital for 100 paupers; this finally fell into ruin. By the nineteenth century the site was a jungle of tumbledown shacks, thieves' kitchens and grimy coal-wharves.

Then along came Richard D'Oyly Carte. He had been producing the early Gilbert and Sullivan operettas with such success that he decided they must have a playhouse of their own. In part of Peter's old grounds, he built the Savoy Theatre, the world's first public building to be entirely lighted by electricity. On opening night, 10 October 1881, before the overture to *Patience*, he stepped out on to the stage and shattered a light bulb, to reassure the audience that there was no danger of fire.

With his theatre flourishing, he set out to revolutionize England's entire social pattern. Even the best English hotels were then looked on merely as convenient necessities for travellers, not as centres for pleasure in their own right. He had, however, seen in the United States superlative hotels which encouraged high society to venture out from behind their closed doors. London, he determined, must have a hotel that would do the same, rivalling the best homes in the land, providing the most modern comforts, the finest cuisine, the most attentive servitors.

His new Savoy Hotel, completed in 1889, was the wonder of the age. With its steel and concrete frame, it was Europe's first fire-proof building. It had its own plant for electric lighting; its own artesian wells; 24-hour room service, and speaking tubes on every floor from which to command it; 'ascending rooms' panelled in red Chinese lacquer; and 70 bathrooms – at a time when London's then most luxurious hotel, the Victoria, had a total of four for 500 guests.

The Savoy's first manager was César Ritz; its first master chef was Escoffier; Johann Strauss at one time led its orchestra, and Anna Pavlova danced in its cabaret. Duchesses, countesses and viscountesses who wouldn't have dreamed of dining in public before, swept into the restaurant. The supreme accolade came from the Prince of Wales, who brought with him an exalted train including his beloved Mrs Keppel and Mrs Langtry, the Jersey Lily. For Bertie, Escoffier created

50 Strand entrance, The Savoy

a suggestively-named dish, *Cuisses de Nymphes à l'Aurore*; but the shapely thighs were those of frogs, their first appearance on an English menu.

Leaders of society, politics and the theatre delighted then as now in the private dining rooms, named *Iolanthe, Mikado, Pinafore* and *Gondoliers*. In front of a mirror in the *Pinafore* room stands a sleek black cat carved of plane wood, whose name is Kaspar. Whenever there is a party of 13 guests anywhere in the hotel Kaspar is taken down from his perch to become the fourteenth guest, and thus ease the worries of the superstitious. A chair is pulled up to the table for him, a napkin tied under his chin, and a complete setting, course by course, laid before him.

Celebrities and the Savoy have always been inseparable. After the opening at Covent Garden of *Manon Lescaut*, Puccini entertained Dame Nellie Melba (Escoffier had already invented Melba toast and *pêche Melba* in her honour). Franz Lehar fêted his cast here after the triumphant first night of *The Merry Widow*. Sir Henry Irving was a permanent resident, and Sarah Bernhardt lived here for a while – and almost died here, from an overdose of sleeping medicine. Tetrazzini bewitched diners by standing on a chair and singing *Home Sweet Home*. Monet, from a bedroom high above the embankment, painted his smudgy, misty impressionist views of the Thames. Marconi made his historic broadcast to the States from the Savoy. Arnold Bennett modelled his *Imperial Palace* on the Savoy, and the hotel owns the original manuscript.

The hotel's style was largely set by Sir George Reeves-Smith, who followed César Ritz and was managing director of the company from 1901 to 1938. He had been managing the Berkeley, and in order to acquire the man, Richard D'Oyly Carte bought the little hotel, which has, ever since, been a member of the Savoy Group. Some people might say that the standards Sir George established are downright finicky. All the Savoy's china, linens and silverplate, are made according to its own demanding specifications. All its beds and mattresses are built in its own workshops, and so comfortable are they that clients often ask to buy them. In a fragrant room below stairs, a dozen girls daily arrange thousands of fresh flowers for use throughout the hotel.

The hotel's annual meetings used to be enlivened by the wit of the late A. P. Herbert who was a minor shareholder in the company. In 1969, he addressed the chairman, Sir Hugh Wontner:

'How fortunate, I often think, Sir, are professions like yours . . . you . . . can say, "This day, as on every day, we welcomed the world; and we made the world happy. From every corner of the globe they came . . . in search of a certain magic which surrounds the name of Savoy. We gave them every courtesy and comfort, good company and good refreshment, and they said, most of them, "Thank you. We will come again." For these benefits they rewarded us with their queer foreign money, which is dear to our rulers.'

X
THE CITY

To OUTSIDERS the area of London known as 'The City' is an enigma. This is how its own ruling body, the corporation, describes it: 'When Londoners talk about "the City" they mean, not Westminster, nor the 32 Boroughs of the Greater London Council, but the "Square Mile" of financial know-how that sits roughly within the lines of the Roman and Medieval walls. It contains not only the "Institutions" – the Bank of England, the Stock Exchange, Lloyd's, the Commodity Markets, etc – but hundreds of small businesses which are "just around the corner", and need to be so, for they are mutually dependent. . . .' The City's business, says the Corporation, is business. It is the most closely knit commercial unit in the world.

As a financial powerhouse, its only match is Wall Street. But unlike Wall Street, the City is fiercely independent of the metropolis which surrounds it. It has its own lord mayor, its own government, its own police force. And the noble cathedral of St Paul's, which stands atop Ludgate Hill looking westward towards Fleet Street (the press is in the City, if not precisely of it), bears the name of the Square Mile's patron saint.

The City's existence as a strong and separate entity is as old as recorded history. In Roman times, fortified and walled, it was already Britain's most important trading centre. Despite Viking and Norse ravages after the Romans left, it remained wealthy, secure and self-confident. When William the Conqueror arrived, he opted, with canny Norman astuteness in business matters, to have its citizens with him rather than against him, and granted them a charter which respected their position and their property. About six decades later, his youngest son, Henry I, accorded them the right (long since lapsed) to select

England's monarch. And King John, even before he was forced to sign Magna Carta, confirmed that London could chose its own mayor; what is more, after he sealed Magna Carta, he included the mayor among the dignitaries who were to see to it that he lived up to his guarantees.

Trade and the City! In addition to its bankers and its brokers, it has buyers and sellers in international, national and local specialized markets of every kind. The diamond men are in Hatton Garden, the fur men in Beaver Hall, the tea merchants and spice dealers in Mincing Lane, the Baltic Exchange, which negotiates some 75 per cent of the world's cargo transport, in St Mary Axe, the meat marketeers at Smithfield and the fishmongers, who claim to have 'everything from everywhere', at Billingsgate beside the Thames. Anthony Sampson in his *Anatomy of Britain* quotes an anonymous jingle:

> *In the City*
> *They sell and buy*
> *And nobody ever*
> *Asks them why.*
> *But since it contents them*
> *To buy and sell,*
> *God forgive them!*
> *They might as well.*

The classic entrance to the City is via the Strand. The spot where its frontiers kiss those of Westminster, at the western end of Fleet Street, is marked by Temple Bar, a cumbersome monument surmounted by a griffin, which stands in the middle of the road. Gates used to bar the entire street, but the last of these (designed by Christopher Wren) was removed in Victoria's time because it had become a traffic bottle-neck. It is at the Griffin that the sovereign must stop before entering the City when she comes on ceremonial visits. She may not proceed until admitted by the lord mayor, who proffers her his sword whether in warning or in homage, no man can say. She touches it, returns it to him and drives on.

A great deal of London's essence is concentrated at this point, some of which feels like the City, even though it falls outside its boundaries. On an island site in mid-street a few dozen yards west of Temple Bar is the church of St Clement Danes; 'oranges and lemons', ring its bells. An eleventh-century church preceded it, begun, as far as is known, for Danish seamen. In the eighteenth century, the present building had many notable parishioners – Burke, Garrick, Goldsmith, Dr Johnson. The doctor, according to an inscription on a pew, attended divine service regularly; yet he wrote of one popular preacher that 'his matter is cold, his manner hot, his voice weak and his action affected.' Johnson's statue stands behind the church, looking down Fleet Street. To his left are the Royal Courts of Justice, where civil cases are tried. On the same side of the street beyond the Bar and beyond Chancery Lane is St Dunstan-in-the-West, which has, in a niche outside, the only statue of the first Elizabeth known to have been created in her lifetime.

Opposite, beside one of London's rare pre-Fire houses, is a narrow cloistered pathway, Middle Temple Lane, which leads into the exclusive legal enclave, the Temple. This is one of London's most bewitching surprises. It includes the Middle and the Inner Temples, two of the four Inns of Court, the only institutions which may prepare a lawyer to practise at the bar. The other two, Lincoln's Inn and Gray's Inn, are nearby, the first off Chancery Lane, the second off Gray's Inn Road, both only the skip of a stone outside the City's lines. They consist of halls of learning, libraries, chambers for barristers and quadrangles of residential flats. These are for the most part occupied by people in the legal profession, but a few outsiders have also been lucky enough to get leases on them.

The inns are leafy oases of tranquillity, as consoling to the town-bruised spirit as the colleges of Oxford or Cambridge. The Temple is probably the most easeful of them all. Courtyard leads under archway to courtyard, a fountain ruminates musically, ivy trails over the mellow brick walls and the lawns roll down to the Victoria Embankment and the river.

At the heart of this peaceful village stands one of the most beautiful houses of worship in the country, and one of the oldest, the round Temple Church, built seven centuries ago in imitation of the round Church of the Holy Sepulchre in Jerusalem. It is from the church that the area derives its name. The connection between the Temple and Jerusalem is direct. After the Holy City was captured in the First Crusade, a group of knights calling themselves the Knights Templar, because their headquarters were on the site of Solomon's Temple, appointed themselves protectors of pilgrims. Some of these men were English, and when they returned home they built their own round church to recall their triumph and their dedication. Some time after the Templars were dissolved in the fourteenth century, part of their property was leased to a group of lawyers and its present use began.

Great cities are filled with invisible frontiers. At Temple Bar there is no hint that a few steps more will bring you into the world of the

51 Lord Mayor's coach

press. Except for the large, pseudo-classical *Daily Telegraph* and the bold, glass-fronted *Daily Express*, the profession does not proclaim itself. But clusters of brass plaques at narrow entrances and signs lettered on windows one flight up declare the presence of countless provincial and foreign newspapers, press bureaus and telegraph agencies.

Fleet Street is, in fact, a generic term, implying the calling as much as the place. Not all the major newspapers are here. Several are in turnings off the street, others as far away as Holborn Circus, Gray's Inn Road and Queen Victoria Street. The London press has a potent sense of identification. It has a church of its own, hidden in a secluded courtyard off the street, St Bride's, a post-Fire Wren building whose spire, delicate tier upon tier, the poet, W. E. Henley, called 'a madrigal in stone'. The press have added bench-ends that commemorate distinguished colleagues of the past. Pepys was baptized here, a most appropriate accident of fate; had he lived a couple of centuries later, he would undoubtedly have been the sharpest of gossip columnists.

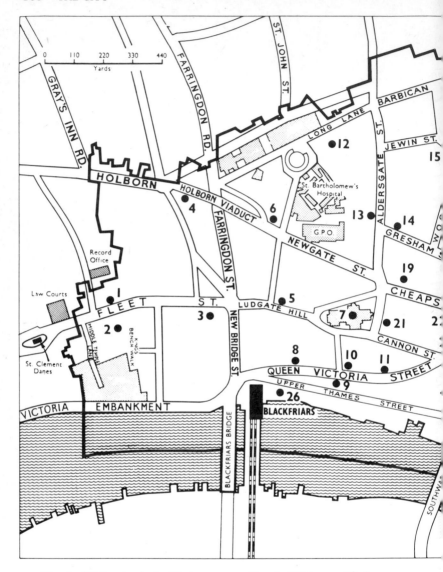

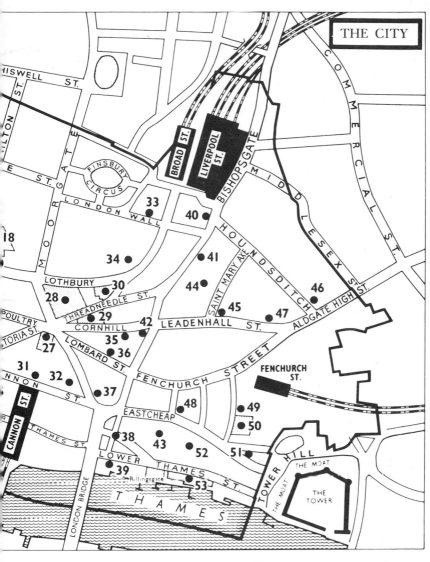

27	Mansion House
28	Bank of England
29	Royal Exchange
30	Stock Exchange
31	Church of St Swithin
32	Church of St Mary Abchurch
33	Church of All Hallows, London Wall
34	Dutch Church, Austin Friars
35	Church of St Michael
36	Church of St Edmund the King
37	Church of St Clement Eastcheap
38	The Monument
39	Church of St Magnus the Martyr
40	Church of St Botolph Without
41	Church of St Ethelburga
42	Church of St Peter
43	Church of St Mary-at-Hill
45	Church of St Andrew Undershaft
46	Church of St Botolph
47	Church of St Katherine Cree
48	Church of St Margaret Pattens
49	Church of St Olave
50	Corn Exchange
51	Church of All Hallows, Barking
52	Church of St Dunstan-in-the-East
53	Customs House

At the eastern end of the street where it enters Ludgate Circus there is on a wall a small plaque dedicated to Edgar Wallace: '. . . to Fleet Street he gave his heart.' When Wallace was sacked from *The Daily Mail* a compassionate colleague asked him what he would do next. He shrugged. 'I don't know. I have a lot of notes and plots in a chest of drawers. I might try to work 'em up into something.' Well, we all know what came of that. But to Fleet Street, Wallace remains one of their own, rather than a whoduniteer. His memorial in St Bride's reads simply, 'Edgar Wallace, reporter'.

The name Fleet is a corruption of the Anglo-Saxon *fléot*, a place where boats floated, a river or stream. The muddy waters of the Fleet River which winds southward from Highgate and Hampstead, had, before they were covered over in the eighteenth century, flowed through what is now Ludgate Circus and what was then a miniature port, clogged with coal barges. All that floats on the Fleet today are ideas, some borne on the stream of ink to the ends of the earth, others sunk into the ancient mud without a trace. You can, however, still catch a glimpse of the river's dark waters through a grating in a sub-cellar of The Cheshire Cheese.

Because Ludgate Hill, as it mounts to St Paul's, veers at an angle, the cathedral seems to stand slightly askew on its summit. Partway up the hill, opening off to the left, is a street with a name that chills any criminal's blood, Old Bailey. At the end of the street is the Bailey itself, formally known as the Central Criminal Courts. The courthouse, crowned by a golden image of Justice blindfolded and holding her scales, stands where once were the ugly walls of Newgate, the most notorious of all English prisons. It was a Hogarthian place, so noisome and so foul that the jail fever emanating from its cells was a constant threat to the entire neighbourhood and above all to the judges who sat upon the cases of the incarcerated. In 1750 the prison disease killed the lord mayor, two judges, an alderman, an under-sheriff and 50 others. To fend off the fever, the floor of the judges' benches and the railings of the prisoners' docks have ever since been strewn with sweet herbs – even in the relatively antiseptic courtrooms of the present Old Bailey – and judges, sheriffs and under-sheriffs all carry nosegays of sweet-smelling English flowers.

The courts of the Old Bailey are open to the public, and a famous trial can play to houses quite as packed as any West End hit. Crowds fill the streets to boo or jeer, just as their ancestors gathered to witness public hangings outside Newgate jail.

But back to St Paul's. The cathedral is, if not the heart, then without doubt the soul of the City. Its black dome with its tall golden cross is visible for many miles. During the Blitz, in December 1940, bombs fell all about it, devastating acres of built-up streets. It was the City's worst disaster since the Great Fire. But there was one important difference. In 1666 old St Paul's crashed in ruins to the ground; in 1940 its successor escaped, although it stood ringed by fire and almost invisible in the smoke that billowed from its burning neighbours. *The Times* reported with understandable feeling:

'The Cathedral has become in these latter years more than ever a symbol of the unconquerable spirit that has sustained the fight. . . . None who saw will ever forget their emotions on the night that London was burning and the dome seemed to ride the sea of fire like a great ship, lifting above smoke and flame the inviolable ensign of the golden cross.'

Some spots seem destined for sanctity, none more so perhaps than the summit of Ludgate Hill. Divine worship of one sort or another is thought to have been celebrated there for almost 2,000 years. Some historians claim that a temple to Diana stood there in Roman times. In the fourth century there was a bishop of St Paul's, Restitutus, which indicates that a Christian place of worship stood hereabouts. Confirmed records exist of Saxon churches built on Ludgate Hill in 604 and in 961. The third on the spot, the pre-Fire cathedral, was begun in Norman times with a gift of stone from William the Conqueror.

Over the next two centuries it became Anglicized architecturally. By the time of the Fire it was in a shameful state of repair. It had survived three strokes of lightning as well as desecration – 'brawlings, murthers, conspiracies' – before the Civil War and was used as cavalry stabling by the Cromwellians. Charles II, on his return called upon Wren to restore it, and the architect proposed so many drastic changes that not much of the old place would have been left even if the Fire had not finished it off.

Enabled by the disaster to make an absolutely fresh start, Wren created his masterpiece. The building began auspiciously when, according to a familiar story, he asked a workman to bring him a scrap of rubble so that he could mark the spot above which the dome's centre would be constructed. The man handed him a chunk of an old gravestone bearing the word '*Resurgam*'.

Wren's pay for the job was niggardly, even by the standards of those days – £200 a year. He himself was frequently up on the scaffolding, causing the Duchess of Marlborough to cluck sympathetically, 'He is dragged up and down in a basket two or three times a week for a paltry £200 a year.' By the time St Paul's was completed, 40 years after he had begun it, he was a frail old man, unable to mount to the top of his dome. His son placed the last stone in the lantern. Wren was buried in St Paul's, with the finest epitaph an architect could possibly desire: *Lector, si monumentum requiris, circumspice* ('Reader, if you seek his monument, look about you').

And so from God to Mammon by way of Cheapside.

There is nothing cheap about Cheapside, nor is there a matching Dearside. The word simply recalls the Old English for barter or market, *ceap*. The street leads towards the unique market-place of London, a concatenation of exchanges, banks, insurance companies, warehouses, wharves – an international mart without parallel.

Walking eastward one passes the church of St Mary-le-Bow, another of Wren's Fire replacements. Its bells are said to have summoned Dick Whittington and his cat back to the City, one of the nicest nonsense fables in London. Only those born within the sound of Bow bells are considered true Cockneys, a condition which is hard to fulfil these days, for although nearly half a million people flock into the City to work each day, it has few residents – perhaps only 7,000 – and hence, few births.

At the end of King Street, a turning off Cheapside, stands the most respected of the City's non-ecclesiastical institutions, Guildhall. Although it still has a medieval crypt, porch and walls, it has been much rebuilt, particularly after damage incurred in both the Fire and the Blitz. An enormous modern wing has recently been added, impressive and spacious if slightly incongruous beside the weather-worn spires and pinnacles, to house administrative offices and a superbly exhaustive – and comfortable – library. Guildhall is to the City what Parliament and Whitehall combined are to the nation. Above the old porch is the City's blazon, which combines the cross of St George, the sword of St Paul and a pair of rampant dragons. Beneath is the City's motto, *Domine Dirige Nos*.

It is reassuring to believe – at least to hope – that the Lord does indeed guide His Worship, the Lord Mayor, his alderman, his council-men and such disparate dependencies and providers of loaves and fishes as the Stock Exchange, the Bank of England, the underwriters at Lloyd's and Messrs Rothschild, Warburg and Baring. Certainly the lord mayor and all his predecessors back to Henry FitzAilwin, who took office in 1191 or 1192, would have been grateful for help of the highest order: the job of running the City is enormous.

The corporation operates through 'the Mayor, Aldermen and

52 North transept, St Paul's cathedral

53 *left* West end of Temple Church

54 *below* Guildhall, showing new extension

Commons of the City of London in Common Council Assembled'. The mayor is elected by his fellow aldermen and serves for one year, during which he not only heads the corporation but is the City's chief magistrate, the admiral of the Port of London, and the City's leading citizen, with the status of an earl. When he summons his quasi-parliament to Guildhall, he is assisted by a bevy of officials with resounding titles: the chamberlain, the remembrancer, the common cryer, the sword bearer. The sword and the mace lie crossed on a table before the lord mayor.

Next to the royal regalia, his are the most splendid of England's symbols of high office. The mace is of silver-gilt and dates from 1735. The sword is 55 years older. His chain of office is a golden collar with enamelled Tudor roses made in the sixteenth century; a dangling sardonyx encircled by diamonds was added in 1799. He also has a jewelled sceptre, part crystal, part gold, the shaft of which is thought to be Saxon and the head of which is known to be fifteenth-century; this he carries at coronations. Perhaps his most fitting piece of ceremonial equipment is the City purse – red, heavily gilt and embroidered, probably Elizabethan – which is handed to him when he assumes office, a tangible reminder that money is the City's business. And he rides in a pageant-filled procession the day after he takes office, in a golden coach which rivals the queen's own.

Before he and his councillors can get down to the nitty-gritty of sewers, traffic control, public health, building codes or whatever, he intones the motto, *Domine Dirige Nos*, which echoes through Guildhall's Great Hall, a vaulted chamber as large as three Wimbledon doubles courts.

Looking down from a pair of brackets, more or less benignly, are Gog and Magog, two grotesque limewood effigies over nine feet tall. Nobody is certain who these creatures are, or why they are there. These two are replacements for an eighteenth-century pair destroyed by the bombs in 1940. And those were successors to even earlier ones made of wicker and pasteboard, which were carried in lord mayoral pageants in the fifteenth and sixteenth centuries. In Elizabethan times they were known as Gogmagog and Corineous, and myth has it that they were the last of a race of giants born of the 33 daughters of the Emperor Diocletian, that they were captured by the legendary Trojan invaders of Britain, chained and made door-porters at Guildhall.

They are quite hideous: one carries a spiked ball on a chain and the other, a shield and spear. Ned Ward, an eighteenth-century tavern keeper who was renowned both as a kindly host and a bawdy wit, wrote of them thus:

55 The Mansion House

'I asked my friend the meaning and design of setting up these two Lubberly Preposterous Figures, for I suppose they had some peculiar end in't? Truly, says my friend, I am wholly ignorant of what they intend by 'em, unless they were set up to show the City what huge Loobies their Forefathers were, or else to frighten stubborn apprentices into obedience for the threat of appearing before two such monstrous logger heads will sooner reform their manners or mould 'em into compliance with their masters' will, than carrying of 'em before my Lord Mayor. . . .'

The Great Hall was at one time used for trials; Lady Jane Grey was condemned to death there. It is now London's premier banqueting hall. Few kings or presidents in the civilized world have not put their knees under its high table.

Beyond Guildhall, Cheapside becomes the Poultry, so-named because that was what used to be sold there, just as a cross-hatching of smaller streets nearby also proclaim their former wares: Honey

56 St Bartholomew-the-Great

Lane, Milk Street, Ironmonger Lane, Wood Street, Bread Street. The Poultry in turn becomes Mansion House Street, and Mansion House Street pours its tide of vehicles into a confluence of eight streets to form one of the most dizzying traffic maelstroms in daytime London.

Remove the buses, lorries, taxis and Rollses, however, and this lopsided triangular site looks remarkably like a Roman forum, with the columned Royal Exchange directly ahead, the columned front of the Mansion House to the right, and more columns on the façade of the Bank of England to the left. It is, perhaps, no coincidence that the forum of Londinium was at just about the same spot.

The Mansion House, an eighteenth-century Renaissance-style building, is the lord mayor's home, his Ten Downing Street. But in some ways it recalls more the Doges' Palace in Venice. Like the palace it combines three functions. It is an official dwelling, it contains a court room where the lord mayor sits as magistrate and it even has a few prison cells. Also, like the Doges' Palace, it has its own adjacent church. But St Stephen Walbrook is no horizon-filling St Mark's; it is concealed modestly in a side street behind the Mansion House and is, externally at least, unassuming.

Although its tower and most of its rough stone walls predate the Fire, it was gutted by the conflagration and rebuilt – needless to say – by Wren. He capped it with a small gem of a dome, but since there are few vantage points from which this can be seen from the outside, it comes as a breathtakingly beautiful surprise when you enter. The story goes that Wren built this dome as a trial run for St Paul's. 'Never,' a nineteenth-century observer wrote of St Stephen, 'was so sweet a kernel in so rough a shell.' In modern times the church became the birthplace and headquarters of the Samaritans, the worldwide organization whose mission is to aid all those 'tempted to suicide or despair'.

The Royal Exchange, one of the City's many Victorian neo-classic structures, and possibly the handsomest of them all, is the third to stand here. The first was built in the sixteenth century by the institution's founder, Sir Thomas Gresham, he who propounded the much-quoted economic theory that bad money drives out good (and he who built the wall overnight down the middle of his garden at Osterley to satisfy Queen Elizabeth's whim). He modelled his exchange on the bourse in Antwerp, with an open courtyard where merchants gathered and a colonnade filled with shops. Atop a column and carved into the stone walls were grasshoppers, Gresham's crest. Although the building lasted barely one hundred years, the sign of the grasshopper has survived – couchant, gilded, alert, acquisitive – on every branch of Martin's Bank, the first of which Gresham is said to have launched. The present Royal Exchange has long since ceased to fulfill its original purpose; it is now used as an art gallery and exhibition centre.

The Bank – it is unnecessary in the City to add 'of England' – is as much the City's keep as the White Tower is the Tower of London's. Its lower two storeys are lit only by interior courtyards; the exterior is windowless, a security measure. Above rise five more storeys of offices, and beneath are three floors of vaults. These contain the national gold reserve in bullion. A bank official, verifying this point, commented wryly, 'Such as it is!'

The Bank has its own printing works for bank notes, and presumably keeps large numbers of singles, fivers, tenners and so on on the premises, which it supplies to ordinary banks. It also influences what was until recently called the 'bank rate', the minimum rate at which

57 Bank of England and Royal Exchange Building

money should be lent. This is decided upon once a week. There used to be an engaging formal ceremony by which the rate was made known: the senior government broker, having been advised by the Bank's governor and court, put on his top hat and walked to the Stock Exchange where, standing on a chair, he proclaimed the percentage to the assembled members. No more, alas. The rate is now given each Friday to the news agencies.

The Bank was found in 1694 to provide William III with £1,000,000 for the war of the Grand Alliance against France. Since then it has come to manage most of the government's monetary affairs, including the national debt. But the government is not its only client. There have always been a few private accounts, and members of the staff are permitted to bank with their employer. Cheques are printed in flowing script, much like those issued by the royal bankers, Coutts and Co. It must be rather a pleasant experience to pay one's gas bill with a cheque drawn on the Bank of England.

Although much of what the City does occurs behind closed doors, two of its longest-established and most colourful exchanges are open to anyone who can persuade himself to get up early enough – the Smithfield meat market near the City's northern border at Farringdon Street, and the fish market at Billingsgate.

Smithfield has no peer in what the trade calls 'bright' (fresh) meat and poultry. So big and busy is it that it even has its own police force. The clients are largely butchers and restaurateurs, but several retail butchers' shops, always crowded, nestle at its fringes. The main market building is long and low, its windows arched, its corners adorned with towers pierced by round apertures – it would be almost too appropriate to use the French phrase, *oeil-de-boeuf* – and surmounted by ribbed domes topped by pierced lanterns.

Smithfield has nothing to do with any historic Mr Smith. The word is a corruption of 'smooth'; in the twelfth century, the market place was described as 'a smooth field where every Friday there is a rendezvous of fine horses to be sold, and in another quarter are placed vendibles of the peasant, swine with their deep flanks and cows and oxen of immense bulk'. You could buy a whole pig or cow then for less than twelve shillings. Tournaments took place there as well, archery contests and public executions. On one dreadful occasion, 200 so-called heretics were burned, and in Victorian times, workmen laying a sewer found an evidential pile of charred bones.

One winter's dawn we were escorted through Smithfield by the then chief meat-buyer of Harrods, a dignified frock-coated gentleman who, in his off moments, is a lay preacher. At his approach the usual profanity of the 'bummarees' – porters – was stilled, though whether out of respect for the Lord or the lordly Harrod's representative, we were unable to determine. We dropped into Smithfield's own pub, The Cock, which opens at 6:30 in the morning. Market men were drinking 'wazzer', a combination of tea and whisky, and consuming monstrous steaks. The unseasonable hour combined with the many carcasses we had just seen swinging from hooks deprived us of any appetite and we looked on queasily.

Across from Smithfield is St Bartholomew-the-Great, which, despite its name, is a very small church. It is, after the chapel of St John in the White Tower, the oldest church in London, with rounded Norman arches and a forest of thick columns. Over its gateway is a house with a half-timbered front, an Elizabethan addition. St Bartholomew was founded by Rahere, a courtier of the first Henry. A Latin manuscript in the British Museum describes him as a self-serving young man who haunted the households of nobles and the palaces of princes, 'where under every elbow of them he spread their cushions with apings and flatterings delectably annointing their eyes, to draw him to their friendships'.

But like Thomas â Becket and Ignatius Loyola, Rahere abandoned the worldly life for the austerities of religion. He journied to Rome where he fell ill and, so the legend goes, had a vision in which he saw himself snatched up by a winged monster and dangled over a bottomless pit. Then St Bartholomew rescued him! In return, the saint enjoined him to build a church in 'Smoothfield'. When he came back to London he did so, a cushion perhaps for the elbow of St Bartholomew, and he died a monk.

Billingsgate spreads along the Thames eastward of London Bridge. Fish has been sold here for almost 300 years, and in the beginning most of it came from the Thames estuary itself. Supplies now reach Billingsgate by air, sea, road and rail – salmon and turbot, sole and catfish, dogfish, crustaceans and coalfish, about 350 tons every day.

In Billingsgate you can see London at its liveliest – and noisiest. The market has always been renowned for foul-mouthed speech, compared to which Smithfield's standard vocabulary seems almost courtly. *The Chronicle History of King Leir*, Shakespeare's source for his *Lear*, spoke of '. . . as bad a tongue . . . as any oyster-wife at Billingsgate hath'. The vituperative porters still carry wooden crates of fish on their heads, and wear protective leather hats so toughly made that they are passed on from father to son. They are said to be modelled on the leather headgear worn by Henry V's archers at Agincourt.

Behind Billingsgate is Pudding Lane, where stood the shop that baked the king's bread that burst into flames and set the whole City alight in 1666. Now anyone would think that if there had to be a monument to commemorate that disaster (the British have a predilection for celebrating dire events: what other nation would have a national festival to recall a national villain like Guy Fawkes?), it would have been set on the precise spot where all the trouble began. Not at all! It is at the corner of Fish Street Hill and Monument Street, a fluted Doric column 202 feet high. And why 202? Because that is the distance of its base *from* the baker's shop. There must be some logic in this somewhere.

Among the thousands of executives bound for the City any weekday morning are 13 whose like and titles exist nowhere else. They are all members of the College of Arms: three Kings of Arms – Garter, the principal, Clarenceux for the south and Norroy for the north; six Heralds – Lancaster, Chester, Richmond, Somerset, Windsor and York; and four Pursuivants – Bluemantle, Rouge Dragon, Rouge Croix and Portcullis. Their master is the Duke of Norfolk, hereditary Grand Marshal of England, and their working home is a graceful red brick building, designed in the mood of Wren, though not by Wren himself. Inside are rooms for the officers, a library and the Grand Marshall's Court, which was founded to adjudicate squabbles over coats-of-arms and family trees. Until recently a black and white cat named Claude used to pad freely about the premises, wearing around her neck a chain bearing the arms of the City of London. She was the last of a line of feline mascots – all black and white (sable and argent, as the college would say) – but traffic in Queen Victoria Street has become too heavy to risk replacing her. Two paintings of Claude hang on the college walls, one of which, the work of a herald, was the institution's Christmas card a few years ago. The college was chartered by Richard III, and the present site granted by Mary I. Charles II declared that the earl marshal was 'the next and immediate officer under Us for determining and ordering all matters touching Arms, Ensigns of Nobility and Chivalry'. Although the college's word is law on working out family genealogies and designing armorial bearings, it is not publicly subsidized, and pays its own way through the rather high fees it charges for its unique and scholarly services.

Despite the fact that the college is thus an eccentric example of private enterprise, its members are all servants of the queen. The earl marshal stage-manages coronations, openings of parliament and state funerals, and his heralds constitute his headquarters staff. They also appear in their emblazoned tabards on ceremonial occasions, irresistibly recalling medieval tournaments or, even more perhaps, the trial of the Knave of Hearts in *Alice in Wonderland*.

Despite the antiquity and the oddity of their calling, the heralds are busier than ever. Families of English origin from all over the world come to them to have their pedigrees established, and commerce and industry have shown a growing delight in displaying coats-of-arms, a custom which began in 1439, when the college confirmed a grant of arms to the Worshipful Company of Drapers. The retail chain of Marks and Spencer stores recently asked the college to design a blazon. It is a gorgeous piece of heraldry, shot through with symbolic representations of the company's business prowess and history. The M & S house journal described it in these words:

'The golden scales in the centre are a symbol of Michael the Archangel and stand for justice and fair trading. The heraldic

pattern on the shield forms the letter "M" for Michael, for Marks and for Manchester where we opened our first shop. The white roses are for Yorkshire, the county home of our first penny bazaar in Leeds. The ladder on the crest derives from Jacob's dream, a symbol of upgrading. The two cornucopiae come from Greek legend and symbolise our merchandise. Supporting the crest are the lion of England and the owl, a symbol of knowledge and wisdom.'

Self-congratulatory, one may say, but after all, there is nothing intrinsically modest either about merchandising or about heraldry.

The City, because it *is* trade and commerce, inevitably conjures up an image of hard-faced men with computers where their hearts should be. The story of what is going on in the new Barbican development negates any such cliché.

After World War II, the City found itself with 63 acres at the northern end of the Square Mile beside the Roman wall, which had been almost completely flattened by Nazi bombs. The area, known as the Barbican – from the 'barbican' or watch-tower over the Cripplegate, part of the Roman fortifications – was now a wilderness. What to do with it? The first instinct of the moneymen was to build business blocks, maximizing the commercial value and swelling the City's coffers through high rates.

But this proposal was turned down by the government at Westminster, and the minister of housing, then Churchill's son-in-law, Duncan Sandys, suggested instead that the Barbican be transformed into a 'genuine residential neighbourhood incorporating schools, shops, open spaces and amenities, even if this means foregoing a more remunerative return on the land.' The corporation agreed, and putting its money where its mouth is, it at first earmarked £15,000,000 for the project, then raised it to £55,000,000. The plan provides for 2,100 residences, a 500-place girls' school, a youth hostel, restaurants, lakes, gardens, traffic-free pedestrian walks and a comprehensive arts centre.

At the edge of the development, at the corner of London Wall and Aldersgate Street, a tower museum has risen, which now houses both Guildhall's museum of London artefacts, including many from the period when it was Londinium, and the old London Museum, which contains more recent historical items and was formerly in Kensington Palace.

Not since Shakespeare's day have the arts had more than the frailest toehold in the City. The first 'first night' since then took place in

1959 when the Mermaid Theatre, constructed inside a bombed Thameside warehouse, opened for business. The new centre, which is expected to be finished in the late 1970s, will include a concert hall for the London Symphony Orchestra, an art gallery, a sculpture court, a library, quarters for the Guildhall School of Music and, most important of all, a theatre as advanced as the National for the Royal Shakespeare Company.

It is a happy thought that, by the end of the present decade, the Bank of England, the Stock Exchange and the lord mayor of London will be treading the same primrose path as did the Zeigfields and the Cochranes – all the fabled impresarios of the past.

XI
MUSEUMS: TREASURES, TROPHIES AND TRIVIA

THERE is a highly individualized species of madness which yeasts in the brains of collectors. London has perhaps 100 museums, large and small, public and private, of assorted varieties, and some, despite the sober efforts of generations of trustees, government officials and scholars, will always be lightly brushed with divine lunacy. Why, for instance, should the British Museum own such disparate items as an Anglo-Saxon pitcher, Captain Scott's diary and a Nigerian carving which depicts a white official whom a former keeper of the ethnography department described as 'sitting on a litter, complete with pith helmet, and looking on rather dyspeptically'?

In the eighteenth century, before the concept of public galleries had yet taken hold, private fanciers amassed and displayed assorted curios, each according to his taste. Don Saltero, a Chelsea innkeeper whose real name was James Salter, had thousands of dubious bits and pieces in his pub – his 'knackatory', as he called it. Richard Steele listed a few in *The Tatler*:

> 'A piece of Queen Catherine's skin; the Pope's candle with which he curses the heretics; a painted ribbon from Jerusalem with which our Saviour was tied to the pillar when scourged; Manna from Canaan; a necklace made of Job's tears; Pontius Pilate's wife's chambermaid's sister's hat.'

At one extreme were the hoarders of such rude and charlatan trivia. At the opposite end in terms of taste, but no less stricken with the mania to surround themselves with 'things', were the exquisites – Charles I and his master paintings; the Hanovers and their libraries; hundreds of wealthy milords who scooped up thousands of foreign

treasures during hundreds of grand tours. The squirrelings of peers and monarchs were at first seen only by those whose birth and rank gave them entrée to the palaces which housed them. In the course of time, however, it was these aristocratic pickings which provided the foundations for some of the nation's most important and authoritative public galleries. But the Don Salteros also contributed, and it was they who created in their ordinary contemporaries an interest in curiosa and memorabilia, a public whose descendants now throng London's museums.

One of the world's finest arrays of *objets d'art* ever privately assembled is the Wallace Collection which now belongs to the nation. The legacy of an extraordinary family, it is contained in Hertford House, a much-restored red brick former home in Manchester Square. Though of inestimable value and gathered together with discernment, it is never-theless idiosyncratic – a magnificent hodge-podge of paintings, majolica, porcelain, European and Oriental armour, a staircase balustrade of wrought iron and bronze forged for the Paris palace of Cardinal Mazarin and, above all, more antique French furniture than any average Frenchman has ever laid eyes on.

The collection was begun with a few Dutch canvasses in the eighteenth century by the Marquess of Hertford, a descendant of Edward Seymour, Duke of Somerset, who was the brother of Henry VIII's third wife, Jane Seymour, and the Protector of her son, King Edward VI. The marquess was also a nephew of Sir Robert Walpole and a political figure in his own right, successively George III's ambassador to France, lord lieutenant of Ireland and lord chamberlain. As if he hadn't been born with all the silver spoons that any man could possibly require, he further enhanced his status by marrying Lady Isabella Fitzroy, daughter of the second Duke of Grafton, and grand-daughter of Charles II by Barbara Villiers, Countess of Castlemaine. Thus the couple combined the blood-lines of the Tudors and the Stuarts.

Their son, the second marquess, also an ambassador and also lord chamberlain, acquired the house which now shelters the family treasures from the estate of the Duke of Manchester, who had built it as a duck-shooting lodge. And it was he who began to purchase major English paintings on a large scale – Romneys, Reynoldses, Downmans, Hoppners. He married twice, and his second wife, Isabella, was painted three times by Romney. She also managed to supplant in the susceptible heart of the Prince Regent his long-suffering and ever-faithful Maria Fitzherbert.

She was, according to one chronicler, 'soft and rounded', and to another, 'fat and blowsy'. Either way, Prinny was smitten, and visited her regularly in the oval drawing-room on the first floor (now Gallery XXII). Under the sway of the marchioness, an ardent Tory, this room blossomed into the most powerful political centre in Britain.

The third marquess was also a celebrated political figure, an MP, an intimate of George IV (the king sent him to Moscow to deliver the Garter to the czar) and a witty, free-spending society leader who became so fascinatingly debauched that Thackeray used him as his model for Lord Steyne in *Vanity Fair*. He enriched the art collection with an open purse. His own fortune was enormous, and he married a second, which his wife, a beautiful Italian dancer, Maria Fagnani, had inherited from her putative father, the fourth Duke of Queensbury. Although they lived mostly in Paris, the marquess owned several London houses, and he bought avidly for them all.

Even more assiduous a collector was his son, the fourth marquess – MP, soldier, diplomat, friend of Napoleon III and, ultimately, recluse. Much of what we see in Manchester Square was acquired by him or for him by his agent and secretary, a mysterious person, Richard Wallace. Besides numerous purchases of the works of French eighteenth-century artists whom the marquess 'rediscovered' – Watteau, Fragonard, Boucher, Greuze – he added a stupefyingly rich selection of more famous masters: nine by Rubens, five by Rembrandt, Frans Hals's *Laughing Cavalier*, two exquisite paintings by Pieter de Hooch, eight Murillos, three Van Dycks, a pair by Velasquez (the list seems endless), Canaletto, Guardi, Luini, Hobbema, Reynolds, Gainsborough, Lawrence.

Who then, was Richard Wallace, whose genius in tracking down art was without rival? His ancestry is more than a touch obscure. His mother called herself Agnes Jackson, although she seems to have been the daughter of a Scottish baronet, Sir Thomas Dunlop Wallace, and had married a man named Bickley. Agnes Whoever-she-was had a love affair with the fourth marquess before he attained his title, and they had a son – first called Richard Jackson, then Richard Wallace and eventually Sir Richard – who was born in London in 1818. He did not meet his father until he was six, after which his mother vanished from the scene. He was taken into the family home in Paris, and in due course became his father's paid secretary and purchasing agent.

They made a good team, for while the marquess was solitary, 'Monsieur Richard' was gregarious, moving in the best salons. When his father died, Richard inherited his entire estate. After the siege of Paris by the Prussians and the rising of the Commune, he removed himself and his resplendent possessions to Manchester Square.

Sir Richard Wallace was in his own right as distinguished as any Hertford in the family line. In Paris he had founded the Hertford British Hospital and won the *Légion d'Honneur*. In England he became a Liberal member of parliament and was a trustee of both the National Gallery and the National Portrait Gallery. He died in Paris in 1890, and his widow, in her will, bestowed the entire Wallace Collection upon the British people, provided that the government should 'agree to give a special site in a central part of London and build thereon a special museum to contain it'. There seemed, however, no good reason to move it at all, so the government bought the lease of Hertford House and later the freehold, and converted stables, coach houses, servants' quarters and private apartments into galleries.

The most famous museum in the British Isles – possibly in existence – is, of course, the British Museum which contains the world's largest library of works in the English language, the most representative examples of the early printed works of other European nations, vast and multifarious arrays of antiquities from every corner of the globe, rare ethnographical and archaeological specimens, sculptures, coins, medals, paintings, drawings. No visitor can ever 'do' the British Museum. It is simply too overwhelming. All one can manage is a judicious sampling – the Elgin Marbles, the Portland Vase, the Easter Island statues, the King's Library, the Rosetta Stone. Even to provide a representative random listing would far more than fill this entire chapter.

The museum was formally instituted on 7 June 1753 in the House of Lords, when King George II on his throne 'adorned with his Crown and Regal Ornaments' gave the royal assent to a bill authorizing the payment of £20,000 for 'the Museum or Collection of Sir Hans Sloane' and for providing 'one general repository' for this as well as for two libraries acquired at the same time. These were the Harleian Collection of Manuscripts, many of them Oriental, which had been assembled by the first and second Earls of Oxford, and the Cottonian Library, the fruits of a painstaking gathering together by Sir Robert Cotton, the Elizabethan antiquary, of literary and historical manuscripts that had been dispersed with the dissolution of the monasteries.

Sir Hans Sloane was an adventurous and innovative physician, among the first to experiment with innoculation against smallpox. As a young man, having served in 1687–8 as physician to the governor of Jamaica, he left the West Indies with 800 exotic plants which apparently survived the journey home, and a guana, a crocodile and a strange yellow snake which, alas, did not. In London he set up a fashionable practice, tended the royal family, was made a baronet by George I and gave his services to the poor for nothing. And all the time he collected, collected, collected – Egyptian, Greek and Roman gods made of gold; mummies; snuff-boxes; vessels 'of agates and Jaspis'; the head of 'a fearfully large whale'; mounted butterflies; insects and reptiles, and 50,000 rare books.

Yet he was a man whom it is difficult wholly to like. His bust in the British Museum is unattractive: he stares coldly from hooded eyes; his thin-lipped slit of a mouth seems to mock; his domed forehead is as high as that of Socrates, his jaw as firm as Wellington's. One admires his scholarship and his energy; he was president of the Royal Society and governor of most of London's hospitals. One respects his generous treatment of penniless patients and his gift of a workhouse for the poor. And one is grateful for the fact that he bestowed upon the Apothecaries, the Physic Garden in Chelsea, now the oldest botanical garden in the country.

But one is appalled by the fact that he, this hoarder of the curious and the evocative, should have destroyed the home in which Sir Thomas More had lived, and which he had bought merely to extend the estate surrounding the Manor House in Chelsea, where he displayed his manifold acquisitions and lived out his last days. And one is repelled by his ruthless career as a property developer. One of his daughters became Lady Cadogan of Oakley, and the other, Mrs George Stanley of Paultons. Cadogan – Oakley – Sloane – Hans – Paultons – all these names figure prominently on the Chelsea map.

It is not surprising to learn that the eclectic Don Saltero was at one time a servant of Sir Hans, and that some of the pub-keeper's gimcracks were cast-offs previously owned by the doctor.

When Sir Hans bequeathed everything he had collected to the nation, in exchange for £20,000 to go to his daughters, he considered that the price represented about a quarter of the true value. Few governments have ever been offered so stupendous a bargain, although Horace Walpole sniffed at it: '. . . hippopotamuses, sharks with one ear, and spiders as big as geese!'

The British Museum was a success story from the start. Bequests and reasonably-priced purchases soon jammed the galleries in its first home, Montague House, which stood in Bloomsbury where the familiar, temple-like building stands today. David Garrick donated his library of 1,000 plays, including many Shakespeare folios. Greek antiquities were bought from Sir William Hamilton, the ambassador to Naples and the notorious Emma's complacent husband. Nelson's victory of the Nile led to a string of Egyptian acquisitions, among them the Rosetta Stone. The Elgin Marbles were bought in 1816, and in 1823 George IV donated his father's 65,000 books, 19,000 pamphlets, maps, prints and drawings.

By the middle of the nineteenth century Montague House had become hopelessly overcrowded, and parliament voted funds for a new museum. But the extensive building programme, which took some 30 years to complete, was outpaced by the constant flow of gifts. The circular domed reading room was fitted into what had been an open inner quadrangle. This was at the instigation of an Italian revolutionary refugee, Antonio Panizzi, who began as a lowly assistant and eventually became principal librarian. In his early days, books were haphazardly catalogued, and they were so numerous that many were simply heaped on the floor in a dark meanly proportioned apartment. Carlyle complained that he often could find no chair and had to work sitting on a ladder.

Panizzi achieved both adequate space (seats for 458 readers) and order out of chaos. In pleading for funds, he had said to a Select Committee of the House, 'I want a poor student to have the same means of indulging his learned curiosity . . . of fathoming the most intricate inquiry, as the richest man in the kingdom.'

In the 1880s, the natural history section was moved to a new home of its own in South Kensington, and in 1905, most of the newspaper library was transferred to a purpose-built repository at Colindale in North London. In 1946, the trustees bought the former Civil Service Commission building in Burlington Gardens to contain the ethnographical department, now known as the Museum of Mankind.

The museum costs the taxpayer about £4,000,000 per year. But the taxpayer is given a great deal gratis through generous annual money bequests. It is pleasing to realize, for instance, that George Bernard Shaw willed one-third of his residual estate for the museum's upkeep, and, therefore, that every time we feel like wandering in to look at a lithely lovely Egyptian cat or at a Greek bronze fashioned before Homer wrote, the royalties of *My Fair Lady* are helping to pay for our delight.

If the entire world's surface were suddenly covered by ice or engulfed by the oceans, and only one scrap of South Kensington were spared, a parallelogram barely one-quarter of a mile broad and less than half a mile long, bounded by Hyde Park on the north, the Cromwell Road on the south, and more or less enclosed between Queen's Gate and Exhibition Road, travellers from another planet could still form a pretty shrewd notion of what human civilization had been all about.

60 *above* Victoria and Albert Museum

61 *right* Aviation Gallery, Science
Museum

Post-cataclysm tourists strolling along these imposing boulevards might fairly conclude that, until disaster overtook us, we were a self-confident lot. Consider those oversized Romanesque, Renaissance and classical façades, those turrets, steeples, spires and finials, the ascending flights of broad and stately steps. The academic institutions, the museums and the enormous circular concert hall, the Albert Hall, into which all these handsome portals open are perhaps the purest expression anywhere of Britain's suberb, almost arrogant, assurance during the final golden years of Victoria's reign.

What a cornucopian era that was – science, moral reform, artistic outpourings, a new and heady sense of the infinite largesse of the globe. In England its apotheosis was the Great Exhibition of 1851, an explosion of human accomplishment whose shock waves spread through many succeeding generations and left their richest residue in South Kensington.

From the corner of the Cromwell Road and Exhibition Road you can see four repositories of knowledge and of expertise – the Science Museum, the Natural History, the Geological with its wealth of fossils and gemstones, and the incomparable Victoria and Albert. The original concept of the V and A, which developed under the direct impetus of the Exhibition, was to assemble fine examples of craftsmanship – ancient and modern, not only from Britain but from wherever it flowered – so that artisans of the nineteenth century could study and profit by their predecessors' examples: leatherwork, ironwork, ceramics, tapestry, costumes, furniture, enamel, woodcarving, architectural design, silversmithing, goldsmithing, engraving, book production, stage design.

The museum is still the haunt of the technician, the professional – the potter, textile-weaver, furniture-maker, costume designer. And there is a constant flow of antiques collectors who consult staff experts to authenticate the period or the maker of a piece of porcelain, a silver spoon, a satinwood table. But the galleries are always thronged with the general public as well. Youngsters crowd through, pointing and chattering, absorbing the human heritage as painlessly as if it were a huge iced lolly. And the rest of us, quiet and meditative, drift from case to case, sensing, however obscurely, that *homo sapiens* isn't quite the twit he often seems to be.

The V and A inevitably straddled the shadow-line between craftsmanship and art, and surged far beyond its original brief with the acquisition or loan of masterpieces in oil painting, watercolour, sculpture and tapestry. It has on display, for instance, the Raphael Cartoons – seven of the original ten – the designs which the Renaissance genius created for tapestries for the Sistine Chapel.

The V and A, like the British Museum, contains too much of too many categories to be gobbled up in a single feast. Its galleries must be taken one by one. The arrangement makes this easy. English and Continental furniture are set forth in period rooms with panelled walls, carved doors and balustrades, gilded and painted ceilings. In the English section you can study the works of Tudor craftsmen whose names are long-forgotten and of later masters whose names are their own hallmarks – Kent, Adam, Chippendale, Sheraton.

The most outlandish piece is the 'Great Bed of Ware', a carved and inlaid oaken specific for insomniacs which dates from about 1580, and is eleven feet, one inch long and ten feet, eight inches wide. Shakespeare had Sir Toby Belch refer to it in *Twelfth Night*: 'As many lies as will lie in the sheet of paper, although the sheet were big enough for the bed of Ware.' It was a tourist attraction as long ago as the eighteenth century, at the Crown Inn, in Ware, Hertfordshire. It is said that once 12 butchers and their wives slept in it in two rows, six couples at the head, and the other six at the foot.

The V and A leaves you awestruck, not only by the diversity of the objects to which man has set his hand over the centuries, but also by the penchant of the British to roam their own country and the world and return with so many crates and shiploads of wonders: sculptures by Donatello; reliefs by della Robbia; a pulpit from a Cairo mosque; Queen Elizabeth I's virginal; a cannon used by the ferocious slave dealer, Tippoo Sahib; the brick front of a railway station; lacquered doors from a palace in Isphahan; a room from Henri IV's hunting lodge; the Ameer of Afghanistan's armchair; the ring Charles I gave to Bishop Juxon on the scaffold; a definitive collection of Wedgwood; theatrical set-models, and costumes dating from the sixteenth century to our own time.

Across from the V and A's side entrance in Exhibition Road is the Science Museum, the brain-child of Prince Albert, and as complete in the fields of science and engineering as is the V and A (of which it was once part) in arts and crafts. To your left as you enter is an exhibit which is very comforting in an unstable century – the pendulum devised by Jean Bernard Léon Foucault, a nineteenth-century physicist. His pendulum hangs freely in a stairwell while a slowly shifting calibrated scale beneath, firmly attached to Mother Earth, proves that she is constantly moving. Foucault's pendulum is both mystical and baffling: since the pendulum itself does not depend from some fixed and distant star but presumably from a hook in the building

62 Natural History Museum

high above our heads, is it not, therefore, also fettered to the earth? Surely it must be. And yet the graduated scale below creeps on as inexorably as Omar Khayyam's moving finger, a miniscule dot (in London, sw7) on the surface of the revolving globe.

There *is* comfort in that stairwell. How happy Galileo would be there. *Eppur si muove.* Indeed!

The Science Museum is filled with confirmation of technical ingenuity. In the transport department stands Stephenson's 'Rocket', the ugly old steam-engine which won its maker £500 in a trial run on the Liverpool and Manchester Railway in 1829. Not far away is a gigantic modern Diesel engine, proof of how far inventiveness has progressed. There are scores of ship models, vessels of war and liners like *Queen Elizabeth, Mauretania* and *Majestic,* to remind us of the spacious days of transatlantic travel.

On the top floor, a Hawker Hunter, a Spitfire and a Messerschmidt dangle from the roof in eternally arrested flight, like mating birds: 'Forever wilt thou love and she be fair!' In another stairwell, a space rocket juts upward, sinisterly kinetic. Throughout the museum are devices in form and moving both express and admirable – fire-engines gorgeously red, with gleaming brass; a sledge used by Shackleton in the Antarctic; handlooms and spinning jennies; a phonograph by Edison; James Watt's experimental engines.

Perhaps the most agreeable thing about the Science Museum is the kind of patrons it attracts – excited boys and girls with mothers and fathers, the fathers especially trying to look as though they understood how all the thumping, pumping, ticking gadgets work. A pretty young mother stopped with her little girl beside a model of Isambard Kingdom Brunel's *SS Great Britain*, the first (1845) screw steamer to cross the Atlantic. The child pointed: 'Mummy, did you ever sail in that?' How little time means to a child, still immune to Monsieur Foucault's haunting, inexorable message.

Time, of course, is the *leit-motif* in South Kensington. In the Natural History Museum are dinosaurs like *diplodocus carnegii*, 85 feet long, and at the other extreme, in size and not geological age, the tiny British shrew-mouse, one of the most miniscule of all God's mammalian creatures. Among the species who inhabit or once inhabited our planet – the mastodon from Missouri, the moa from New Zealand, the giant elk from the bogs of Ireland, whales and humming birds – there is a slice of a Californian sequoia, the variety called Big Tree. Since sequoias can live for four or five thousand years, this one must have been cut down in its salad days, for it has only 1,335 rings and a diameter of 15 feet. Though merely a sapling as sequoias go, it makes South Kensington seem transitory.

If this corner of London *in toto* is an encyclopedia, then the National Gallery, looking down through its columns at the spread of Trafalgar Square, is in itself an anthology. The National, with some 2,000 pictures representing a cross-section of the major schools of art, has been called 'probably the most choice and thorough in the world'.

The long, low building, with its little dome and its pair of perky pepper-pot turrets (they earned it the nickname of 'the national cruet-stand' in its early days) is more amusing and inviting than overawing. Despite its dignified columns, which were forced upon the architect because they had been left over when Carlton House was demolished and the authorities didn't know what else to do with them, the National does not seek to impress. Nelson's column and the imperial lions in the square below do that very nicely.

Nobody enters on tiptoe or speaks in a hushed voice. The salons are always crowded. There is a pleasing coffee-house babble of

conversation; bearded and tight-jeaned art students sketch; boy picks up girl; crocodiles of school-kids march in and out giggling naughtily at the nudes, and the footsore collapse on to padded benches.

The National began in 1824 when John Julius Angerstein, a rich Russian merchant who had settled in England, died, leaving in his home in Pall Mall 38 pictures including Titian's *Venus and Adonis*, Rubens' *Rape of the Sabines* and two Rembrandts, *The Woman Taken in Adultery* and *The Adoration of the Shepherds*. At that time England had no national art museum, and Sir George Beaumont, himself a connoisseur and collector, persuaded the prime minister, Lord Liverpool, to purchase the Angerstein pictures. They cost the exchequer £57,000, an extraordinary buy on their own, and made even more so by the fact that Sir George had promised to donate his own paintings to the nation if the government would pay for the Angersteins.

The separate schools of art, paintings from Italy, Spain, England, France, Germany, Holland and Flanders, are arranged chronologically. In the case of Italy, subdivisions are also geographical: Venice, Bologna, Umbria, Milan, Florence, Padua, Ferrara, Siena, Parma and Verona. There are few Italian collections anywhere, including those in Italy, so comprehensive, and nowhere outside the Rijksmuseum in Amsterdam is there a better show of Rembrandts.

In the British section, one room is devoted entirely to portraits, a fact which may well confuse, since directly behind the National there is a separate smaller institution, the National Portrait Gallery. Why should two galleries side by side contain what seems to be repetitive? The answer is simple. While in the National the emphasis is on the genius and fame of the painter, in its neighbour the criterion is the historical importance of the sitter.

The National Portrait Gallery, which was founded by act of parliament in 1856, is a pictorial dictionary of national biography. It contains about 8,000 pictures, many of which portray anywhere from two or three to dozens, even hundreds, of personalities – the House of Commons in session, for instance, or coronation scenes. Thus the number of significant faces available to the student, the historian or the idly interested is, by the gallery's reckoning, between 40,000 and 50,000.

The Tate Gallery, in Grosvenor Road overlooking the Thames, on a site where a prison, the Millbank, once stood, is the liveliest and most fashionable of London's museums. It was begun in 1889, when the sugar-refining magnate Sir Henry Tate gave the nation 65 paintings plus £80,000 with which to house them. The original

63 National Gallery from Trafalgar Square

intention was that the museum should be confined to the best in British art, and its official title is the National Gallery of British Art. But the definition of its contents created a dilemma from the start. The cream of early British paintings – Reynolds, Gainsborough, Romney, Crome, Constable – were already in the National Gallery. It was then decided that the Tate should hang only 'modern' British pictures. But what exactly was modern? How far back did modern go? And if one allowed oneself to be fettered by the word, how representative could the new museum become? Finally a compromise was reached: the National would part with some of its precious British canvasses to help the Tate fulfill its originally-designated role.

Then in 1910, Sir Joseph Duveen paid for the construction of a wing to house the works of Turner, for which the National had inadequate space. If the Tate owned nothing but these Turners, it would be worth crossing the globe to see – nearly 300 paintings, finished and unfinished, and about 20,000 sketches and drawings. To wander through the galleries where they hang – one might better say 'to drift', for Turner's smoky palette produces the effect of earth adrift in the universe – is to be absorbed into the very heart of an artist. Most painters are finite: one merely looks on. Turner is infinite, and one is made a part of his bewitched world.

But the Tate has more, much more – a breathtaking display of the eerily unbelievable works of William Blake, and a superlative collection of Pre-Raphaelites: Ford Madox Brown, Holman Hunt, Sir John Millais, Dante Gabriel Rossetti, Burne-Jones.

With the passage of the years, the Tate's directors had begun to wonder why they should not open their doors to foreign works as well. So in came an assortment including Degas, Renoir, Manet, Monet, Cézanne, Seurat, Sisley, Van Gogh – some willed by Sir Hugh Lane, the Irish collector, others given by Samual Courtauld, the industrialist. (There is a separate and superb Impressionist and post-Impressionist collection in the Courtauld Institute, Woburn Place, Bloomsbury.)

For decades, the museum has welcomed every kind of 'modern' art, from Whistler and Sargent to Epstein and Giacometti through Jackson Pollock down to the latest pop works of the New York school, the Warhols, Lichtensteins and so on. This anything-goes policy has frequently involved the gallery in controversy. As this chapter is being written, the director, a pleasant Scot named Sir Norman Reid, is embroiled in a pyrotechnic squabble over his decision to buy an untitled American work by Carl Andre described simply as '120 fire-bricks 5 in. × $90\frac{1}{4}$ in. × 27 in.'. The Affair of the Tate Bricks has created bewilderment, anger and belly-laughs. Was the museum's public

64 Tate Gallery, Millbank

being conned?

The public didn't seem to think so. Concurrently, they were streaming in in their thousands – some 230,000 during the first eight weeks of an authoritative Constable exhibition assembled to celebrate the bicentenary of the artist's birth. Say what one will about the bricks, the fact remains that not to keep abreast of the Tate's activities is to lose touch not alone with British art, but with the entire international art scene.

It would be hard for a professional or amateur in any field, from aviation to poetry, needlework to law, not to find in London a museum or exhibit devoted to his speciality. Goldsmiths and silversmiths can see the finest works in their field (in addition to those at the V and A) at the Goldsmiths' Hall in the City, which has more plate and jewellery, modern and antique, including the silver-gilt cup from which Elizabeth I is believed to have drunk after her coronation, than anywhere else in the kingdom. Pharmacists will find antique mortars and pestles at the Pharmaceutical Society's headquarters in Lambeth High Street. In a disused church in Brentford High Street is the British Piano and Musical Museum. Typographical equipment is in St Bride's Institute off Fleet Street; cricketing memorabilia at Lord's; stamps in the National Postal Museum; weapons in the Imperial War Museum in Lambeth; TV paraphernalia in the Television Gallery in the Brompton Road; historic toys and dolls' houses, and a great deal more, in the Bethnal Green Museum (a branch of the V and A) in the East End, and period rooms and furniture in the Geffrye (also in the East End), an intimate museum installed in a row of eighteenth-century almshouses.

One of the most vividly alive places of all is the deadly-sounding Public Record Office in Chancery Lane, a mock Tudor/Gothic building which is the repository of the nation's archives. For the most part, it serves scholars who come on readers' tickets to pore over historical documents. There is also a museum open to the public in which, on small scraps of paper or great rolls of parchment, Britain's story is illuminated by the jotting hand or the troubled heart.

Thus, a letter from Essex to Elizabeth: 'Hast, paper, to thatt happy presence whence only unhappy I am banished. Kiss that fayre correcting hand which layes new plasters to my lighter hirtes, butt to my greatest woond applyeth nothing. Say thou cummest from shaming, languishing, despayring S.X.'

A letter from the outcast Wolsey to Henry VIII begs 'grace, mercy, remissyon and pardon' for 'the King's poore, hevy and wrechyd prest'.

65 Domesday Book, in the Public Record Office

There is a trumpet call, brazen with victory, from Sir Francis Drake writing aboard *Revenge*, who exults that God gave 'us a good day in forcing the enemy so far to leeward' and predicts that 'the Prince of Parma and the Duke of Sedonya shall not shake handes this fewe days'. There is the confession of Guy Fawkes of his part in the Gunpowder Plot, a letter from George Washington to his 'great and good friend' George III, written long after the revolutionary guns had stilled. There is a papal bull, the seal designed by Benvenuto Cellini, confirming Henry VIII as 'Defender of the Faith' and the log of *Victory* detailing the Battle of Trafalgar. These are not footnotes to history; they are history itself.

The most precious object is the Domesday Book, the incredibly detailed survey of England compiled in 1086 by order of William the Conqueror, and recorded in monkish calligraphy in two vellum-bound volumes. The ownership of every acre of land was ascertained by the king's agents from deeds of possession and the testimony of the land-owning gentry. This listing of real estate, dry as a telephone directory, conceals more than it reveals; it constitutes an implicit recognition of the owners' importance as a class, 'all the land-holding men of any account throughout England, whosoever men they were'. These gentry, in Churchill's view, were recognized by William as they had been by his Saxon predecessors as the flesh-and-blood buttresses which sustained government. From the Conqueror's royal acknowledgement of their stature and influence grew the concept of king and people bound together, and hence, in time, the theory and practice of constitutional and parliamentary government. The spirit that still moves the people of England is all there, in those two old volumes in Chancery Lane.

INDEX